The Super Couple:
A Formula for Extreme
Happiness in Marriage
by Christine M. Bacon, Ph.D.

© Copyright 2015 Christine M. Bacon, Ph.D.

ISBN 978-1-63393-201-2

Published by

BACON
Life, sunnyside up.

CMB Communication, Inc.
1385 Fordham Dr. Ste. 105-170
Virginia Beach, VA 23464
(757)343-0368

THE
SUPER
COUPLE

A formula for
EXTREME HAPPINESS
in
MARRIAGE

CHRISTINE M. BACON, PH.D.

TABLE OF CONTENTS

ACKNOWLEDGEMENTS

After five years devoted to this labor of love (a lifetime really) I struggle with the appropriate words to convey my deepest appreciation for all who contributed to the success of *The Super Couple*. Nonetheless, I will do my best to be both succinct and comprehensive.

First, Martha and Ken—Mom and Dad—you were the first to encourage me as a little girl by always saying "you can do anything you put your mind to" and "I know you're going to do something big with your life someday." You never let me doubt myself. You sacrificed all. Your love and support were never in doubt. Thank you for tolerating my tears of frustration and savoring my simple successes along the way. I love you as much as a daughter can possibly love a parent.

Second, my supporters. By this I mean all of you who supported me *emotionally* by never letting me doubt myself, *financially* by sacrificing your hard-earned dollars in gifts all too generous just because you believed in me and the message of this book, and *spiritually* through your constant prayers that kept me sane, focused, and energized. I felt blanketed by the covering of peace and grace. I deserved none of these things yet you gave them without reserve and for that I remain deeply humbled. Though I promised myself I'd name no names or I'd have to name all names I feel compelled to acknowledge specifically Crystal Cameron-Schaad—my amazing accountability partner—for supporting me in all three ways and for forcing my forward momentum whenever life's excuses beckoned my attention elsewhere. You refused to let me flounder or fail. You have been a blessing beyond compare.

Third, to the man who said "Sure, go ahead and write this book—as long as my name isn't in it" and yet became my story's main character. You, Dan, are the main character in my life and I treasure your love and commitment without which this book could never have been written. Together you and I have shown the world that Super really is possible for any couple that seeks to attain it. How many days, dates, and dinners have you sacrificed? Too many to be counted, for sure. But I will spend my lifetime attempting to repay your sacrifices. I love you dearly.

Finally, I acknowledge my God in heaven. You Who brought me to it vowed you'd pull me through it and You certainly did—beyond anything I could have ever conceived. I was not perfect but I did my best. I answered Your call. I wrote the book. The rest I leave in Your mighty hands. To You alone be the Glory!

PREFACE: THE SUPER COUPLE

Ever since I was a young teen—likely right after hormones began to kick in—I have found myself interested in the current subject matter: why some couples seem to remain extremely happily married while others don't. I am certain it wasn't to the degree that it is now—a degree I would label as a passion or even an obsession—but clearly, in a meaningful way that has stood out in my mind. It was more than three decades later that the label *Super Couples* was given to these special couples. (Little did I know that my own marriage would later fuel this obsession because mine was anything but Super.) As a teen, I had labeled these couples as "cute." You know the kind. I only need give one or two sentences of description and you, too, will say, "Oh, I know a couple just like the ones you're talking about! They're so in love! They'd be perfect for your study!" I know this because nearly every time I articulate my definition of a *Super Couple* this is the response I receive.

Now my description may not sound too academic or formal, especially for one holding a Doctorate in Marriage Communication, but that's deliberate. We don't need heady theoretical descriptions. We need something we understand

and something that works—something that we can apply to our everyday lives and marriages in a meaningful and passionate way. This has seemingly been my mantra throughout life without even my realizing it until recent years. That is, what's the point of knowing this intellectually stimulating stuff if you can't give me an example and better yet, give me some specific instructions on how I should apply it or what I should do differently?

My passion for *your* extremely happy marriage runs deep because it was born out of my passion for my own marriage—the extremely happy marriage that I, too, yearned for but did not have...yet. My marriage began in 1983 like most other marriages. We were passionately in love:

Me: "Oh, I love you!"

Him: "No, no I love you more!"

Me: "Oh I can't live without you!"

Him: "I never want to spend a day apart from you!"

Both: "I can't wait until I get to wake up next to you every single day for the rest of my life!"

You get the picture. I remember the days well when my young Navy boyfriend was so many states away from me and all I thought about nearly every minute of every day was being with him again. Every thought in my head and every cell in my body were constantly focused on this handsome young suitor and the next time I could hear his voice, see his face or, best of all, *be* in his arms again. It was a joyful anguish every young lover has likely endured.

I recall begging my mother to let me have my own phone line in my room so that I didn't have to share a line with any of my siblings once my lover did call. And when he did call we would sit on the phone for hours—literally hours—sometimes just breathing while no words were spoken. Though we'd run out of words, it was as if we were somehow closer to each other through that phone line than we were if we'd hang up. We took in all we could get of each other. I remember the first month my phone bill was $337! Remember, this was 1983 and that was *a lot* of money. My mother hit the roof "You could have bought a washing machine with that money!" The next month she yelled "And *that* was the dryer!" This pattern continued for about two and a half months, but soon thereafter the pain of separation would end as I happily married my lover on August 3, 1983. Oh how I loved that man! And I am certain that he loved me. As I look back nearly three decades I can remember no other time in my life that I was as blissfully happy as I was those few short months my young suitor courted me.

Ok, this book is not about me. Well, it's not *all* about me. It is about you. It is about you, your marriage, and the possibility of you, too, becoming a Super Couple. However, to tell you how to do so, how to *be* so, I must use my own marriage as an example... of what *not* to do.

In August of 1987—two daughters and four anniversaries later—I left my husband. I left him because I *hated* him and no longer felt joy at being in the same room with him but rather felt only pain—deep and miserable pain. Allow me to not yet divulge the causes of that deep pain here as they will be chronicled throughout the following chapters. Suffice it to say divorce seemed the only option. Well, actually it was the second option. Amidst my hate, I shamefully prayed for him to die. (Everyone pities a widow you know, but a divorcee'...not so much.) Know that I am not proud of those words today, but who would I be if I weren't totally honest?

We were separated for four years and "reconciled" in 1991. We were still unhappy. Well, I was, but I'll explain more of that later. Some years later and already into my formal education in the field of marriage, I was conversing with a male colleague of my husband—a very intelligent and rather high ranking and educated military officer. Somehow the conversation turned to marital infidelity and I stated that "Fifty percent of all marriages that endure infidelity go on to survive and often thrive" to which this man replied "That's a bunch of crap. I don't know a single marriage that has survived infidelity!"

I remember that day nearly two decades ago as if it were yesterday. I remember it clearly because his statement silenced me (a grand feat in and of itself)—but not because of what you may think. I was silent because I wanted to exclaim "Well, *mine* has!" But I did not. I remained silent. My husband is an extremely private man who I knew would be devastated if hurtful marital "laundry" were to be exposed publicly. (Kind of ironic to be sharing it instead with thousands of readers decades later through a book detailing not only this marital trial but nearly every private aspect of our marriage as well. *Sorry Dan, for better or for worse. Right?*) I've often thought of that conversation over the years. As it replayed in my mind's eye I'd begun to conclude "Well, how *would* he have known? Who would tell the truth? Who wants to be the first to broadcast his or her failures—especially one of this magnitude?" Then I understood why my friend had not known. Someone needed to be transparent and I'm guessing you've figured out that that "someone" is going to be me.

Many years, a Ph.D., numerous seminars and marriage clients later, I can still look around within my own private circles of clients, colleagues, friends, family members and I *know* which of these couples have had to endure infidelity while most others around them are just as oblivious as my officer friend was decades earlier. I know who they are because they shared with me the pain as they were experiencing it—whether they were the betrayer or the betrayed. And to be honest, of those that have shared their stories of infidelity and marital struggles with me, most are still married today—and happily too. Going through my mental Rolodex I've calculated more than 75 to 90 percent. But while this book is written, in part, *for* you and those who have struggled at understanding what it takes just to make a marriage work (let alone be happy or very happy), it is written *about* those married couples that are not only happy but *extremely happy*.

Extremely...

My doctoral dissertation was on humor and marriage. For five years I was devoted to and entrenched in researching and writing about how humor is used in the marital relationship. It was a great study, and not only did I learn a lot from it, I had a lot of fun writing it. It was a quantitative study, which meant gathering information from a large quantity of couples in the form of a survey to see what patterns emerged and what "new knowledge" could be garnered. As such, nearly eighty questions on the survey pertained specifically to how humor was used in their marriages: How often do you and your spouse laugh together? Does my spouse appreciate my sense of humor? Do I ever use humor in a manner that hurts my spouse? One question on the survey did not pertain to the use of humor in the marital relationship at all but rather simply the overall quality of the relationship. It asked for each spouse to rate the general happiness of his or her marriage on a scale from extremely unhappy, very unhappy, and unhappy, to happy, very happy, extremely happy, and perfect. More than six hundred respondents answered this question and the results amazed me. Seven persons checked "perfect," which I figured were simply newlywed couples who were still having sex three times a day so I smiled and mentally disregarded the accuracy of their response to this question. However, a large number of people—a huge thirty-five percent—checked "extremely happy" and, I must admit, *that* amazed me more.

Extremely happy? What does that mean? I was still hoping to get to "happy" and yet this considerable-sized group of spouses rated their marriages as extremely happy. Wow. Was this an anomaly or was there something bigger going on here of which I was not aware? After all, hasn't it been professed for the past several decades that fifty percent of all marriages failed or were going to fail?

I finished my dissertation later that year but this question and these responses haunted me. *Extremely happy!* They never left my mind. Like that young girl enthralled with those "cute couples" so many decades earlier, I couldn't let go of what this might mean for me, for others, for my concept of marriage, for my concept of those "lucky few" who were so blessed to have found their so-called "soul mates" and of course then for the rest of us who considered ourselves much less lucky in love. *Gosh, I wish I were extremely happy in my marriage. I guess I'm just stuck with this less-than-perfect man and this painful, less-than-perfect marriage. Oh well, I should have picked "the right guy." I wish I'd have picked my one-in-a-million rather than my one-in-one hundred. But I didn't. So deal with it.*

Life went on. On October 25th of that same year my cousin lost her husband of twenty years to cancer. He was only forty-four. I was fortunate enough to be able to travel north to spend a week with her to talk, to listen, and to hopefully—in some small way—help her deal with her grief. We'd talk for hours. Though she was my first cousin and I knew her well, I'd only met her husband twice, as they lived five hundred miles away.

I'd first met Frank on their wedding day and again a decade later during a vacation. I hadn't seen him again apart from a few of his posts on Facebook. But that was it for our "relationship." While talking of her life, her marriage, her husband, and her loss I began to pick up on some of the things my cousin was saying. I began to gain a deeper sense of what her marriage was like through the stories she shared and the way in which she shared them. Finally, I interrupted:

"Maryann, were you and Frank one of those..."

"Super Couples?"

"Yeah."

"Oh yeah. Frank and I, it seemed, never left high school. We would go out of our way to see who could be nicer to the other. Who could beat the other in our friendly but unspoken competition to be the best spouse to the other. I remember once he was having a particularly rotten day. I could tell by the way he sounded on the phone that afternoon. You can always tell. So I decided I would do my best to try and help him feel better about his day's stressors. I went to the store and got everything I needed to prepare his favorite meal. Now I didn't especially *like* cooking but I knew what Frank liked. Just before he came home I had the meal completed, the table spread, and couldn't wait for him to come through the door. I was all excited for him to come home from work and I knew he'd be surprised and happy. Now I must tell you, my favorite candy is peanut butter cups and Frank used to try to make it a point every holiday to get me the latest seasonal peanut butter cup shape before I saw them myself—bunnies at Easter, Christmas trees in December and so on. Didn't it figure though, just when I thought I was going to surprise him, Frank walked in the door and behind his back were three peanut butter cups. As he threw them on the table in front of me I said 'Dang it Frank! You did it again! ... and neither of us won the competition'."

But then again, it seems they'd both won. Maryann and Frank were a *Super Couple*, and thank you Maryann for the title of this book as it seems so appropriate for couples such as yours— couples that seemed stronger, more loving, more passionate, more...well...super in their love for one another. Maryann and Frank's "superness," like that of all the couples interviewed, will help to beget a culture of Super Couples because I learned that Super Couples are not accidental. They are made and are very intentional. This, my readers is the music to your ears you've likely been searching for and hoping to hear. The same music *I* had been hoping to hear.

As I began my research I set out to discover one of two things: did these *Super Couples* have something special that most others didn't have? Did they happen to find their so-called soul mates? Did they simply just get lucky and "sucks to be you" for all the rest of us who were stuck in mediocre marriages or worse yet, marriages like mine that were *troubled?* Twenty-five years into my own marriage and I needed to know. I just *had* to know! Please, dear God! If there is a formula please help me to discover it. I must say that though I had *hoped* to discover the latter, I *expected* to find the former: they just got lucky. (Now there's an optimist for you ☺) But I was wrong—*very* wrong! It is not who couples *are* but rather what couples *do,* what they *say,* and how they interact that makes them super. And therein lies the purpose of this book: to teach you how to become a Super Couple—to present to you the formula, if you will, so that you, too, can import these strategies into your marriage and check the "extremely happy" box...or even the "perfect" box as so many of my Super Couples do. If you've already discounted this possibility in your mind for your own marriage ever becoming Super because you are currently checking the "extremely unhappy box" don't you dare close this book, for it is written even more passionately for you than for those who have never struggled. Remember, this book is written by someone who once *hated* and is now extremely happy with her spouse. That's *right. I haven't told you about the good part yet. But I will. Dan and I followed the formula and extreme happiness followed.* Rest assured, I *know* the depth of your pain. But there is one last thing I wanted to share before I share that formula.

When I was a young bride I remember having a conversation with an older woman—one who'd been married for well over a decade or two. I can't remember specifically what the conversation was about but it must have been about some aspect of relationships or marriage because what she said to me cut me like a knife and has stuck with me all these decades later. She basically told me to grow up and get over myself if I expected the butterflies to last forever—that it was simply a ridiculous and childish notion. I had always been taught to respect my elders and so normally, in any other context, I likely would have listened, let the "new knowledge" she shared with me deflate me, and simply pick myself up and move on. But call me crazy, an idealist, naïve, or whatever, something about that comment was very unsettling and, with all due respect to her age and marital "wisdom," I didn't buy it. I just couldn't. How could I ever not feel for my husband the wonderful things I felt about him at that very moment? How could it possibly go away? *Maybe for you, Lady, but Dan and I are different! He's awesome and you must have just married the wrong guy.* Anyway, we know how *that story* almost ended.

I can confidently say that that well-meaning woman thirty years ago was wrong and I have research to prove it. The butterflies *do* come back! I know this because one hundred percent of those interviewed have informed me that they do (both husbands and wives), and that those more mature butterflies are even better than they were when their love was young and immature. Their hearts still melt. They still get goosebumps. And their sex lives— though different—are much more passionate and rewarding than they ever were on their wedding days.

So, believe me or disagree if you choose. What this book does is analyze the ethnographic research garnered through interviewing more than fifty Super Couples and converts their words and stories into the Super Couple formula so that you, too, may one day attain what on your wedding day you believed to be possible—happily ever after.

SUPER DOES NOT MEAN PERFECT

I suppose it's my fault that whenever I begin talking about Super Couples that at some point someone will correct me or assert, *"I don't think there is such a thing. I mean no one has a perfect marriage. They must be lying or exaggerating."* So let me start out by saying that in no way am I trying to communicate that these couples or any couple for that matter have been struggle free or argument free. Each and every one of these couples would be the first to admit that they definitely have had their fair share of difficulties. One wife was a cabinet slammer. One was a screamer. All had their own personality quirks that caused them to respond in a manner that was not always an "appropriate" means of expressing one's anger, hurt, or disappointment. These were definitely not perfect couples because there are no perfect people.

But remember, these couples were considered to be "Super" because others looked at their marriages from the outside in and saw something they felt was *different,* something special or something they didn't see in their own or most other marriages. From the inside, too, these couples would have to agree—whether or not they were able to put a label on it—that they did, in fact, have something special. Many would even humbly remark, "Oh we're not super, we're just very, very super in our love for one another!"

Yet, I must admit that there did exist for me—and for many others—a subconscious elevation of these couples just a bit to a level that could be considered a marital pedestal. It was protocol to say, "Of course no one is perfect. I know that. I am sure these couples have struggles." But deep down, if I were to be honest, I felt as if they were somehow immune to the "falling out of love" that the rest of the world experienced. It just wasn't possible for them. Marriage came easy. I now know that this faulty idealization of their relationships was part of the problem. Actually believing other couples are "perfect" or somehow just haven't experienced any struggles or difficulties is a huge contributor to the problem in the first place. For instance, I can think of one specific couple who I believed to be a Super Couple from the outside looking in. I envisioned this couple and all other Super Couples coming home with their hearts pounding, looking into the other's eyes, hanging on their every word, and just continually smiling and laughing. Even as they worked through finances and kids these couples must not have raised their voices nor ever gotten frustrated blah, blah, blah. Once I realized that even these couples got irritated with their spouses (but it was rather their decision to not get mean, nasty, or hold grudges etc. that made them different) it allowed me to see that even the most romanticized couples still had to work to be Super and remain Super. Though imperfect, I want this to give you hope for what Super will look like in your marriage—it's good— but most importantly I want to make the vision of what a Super Couple really is more, well, real. These couples are the cream of the crop, the best of the best. But once I realized they weren't lying in bed making mad passionate love all day but that they still lived very normal lives, it had a psychological leveling effect and made the goal of Super Couple a much more attainable goal.

So, please understand, Super, as it is used here, does not mean perfect. But still, after observing and analyzing nearly one hundred couples, it became obvious that each would recite similar phrases about their spouses or repeat similar sentences to me at some point during their interviews. One such phrase I heard from nearly every Super Wife was "I adore my husband!"

That always warmed my heart and, I must admit, reminded me that I was not yet super in my own marriage because to my knowledge I had never uttered that phrase about my spouse. If I had, it would have been at some point in the first year of our marriage (or even before that) when I truly did adore him and was so head-over-heels in love with him that he and I eloped on a Wednesday afternoon with no fanfare whatsoever just because we couldn't stand the thought of not being together every moment of every day. But to *adore* someone ten, twenty, or fifty years into one's marriage is altogether uncommon and absolutely extraordinary.

But before I discuss adoration and those things I actually found that all Super Couples have in common I will begin by telling you first what I *expected* to hear from these couples, followed by that which I *actually heard* in my interviews. Afterwards, I will present to you something that is likely to shock you as much as it did me and that is what Super Couples did *not* list as essential to marital superness. As you follow through the passionate pages of this research I am certain that the Super Couple formula will begin to take shape before your very eyes as it did mine over the many months and years that I was so privileged as to be able to analyze these couples' loves and lives. However, in order to alleviate any potential question or lack of clarity the Super Couple formula will then be spelled out— literally—so that you can then begin to put it to practice in your own marriage. My hope is that once you and your spouse have made it to "Super" (and you will) that you will contact me in order to share your story as well. Who knows? Your journey may one day be, like those of all the couples whose relationships are chronicled between these covers, responsible for getting others to "Super" too.

Part I:

WHAT I THOUGHT I'D HEAR

Faulty assumptions aren't as bad as they might initially sound. As a matter of fact, assumptions are the basis for all research and remain assumptions until they are either proven or disproven. Assumptions aren't just pulled out of the air, but rather are usually based on observation of things, people, and events before those assumptions are formed. Who can fault the initial assumption that our earth was flat? It looks pretty flat to me! And I certainly don't feel myself spinning every day as we circle the sun. But the guy who actually discovered that our earth is round had to begin somewhere. Setting out to discover whether or not the earth was flat was a great place to start. And we all know how that ended.

But seriously, in order to discover the truth about Super marriages we had to start with our assumptions...most of which were found to be faulty or, at best, misunderstood. Additionally, these assumptions were not uniquely held by Christine Bacon and a few others, but rather, these assumptions are commonly held by the populous as is witnessed through everyday conversations and mediated depictions of other "Super Couples." I mean seriously, Brad and Angelina couldn't possibly have ever been anything but happy and in love. Right? They are always smiling when we see them. So clearly there is always peace in their home too. *WARNING: the previous sentence was sarcasm. Please refrain from any unintended belief in its contents. Belief in the aforementioned statement is hazardous to your marital health.* ☺

This chapter is a compilation of some of the most often cited and believed, yet erroneous, assumptions of what Super Couples have that everyone else does not. This is not meant to be a comprehensive list but rather, it contains those assumptions that are often most insidious in their ability to really sidetrack couples by causing them to focus on issues that have relatively little contribution to the attainment of Superness. They are the same assumptions that poisoned my own thinking and marriage and almost led to its demise. But they were faulty. Here is the first.

FAULTY ASSUMPTION 1:
THEY GOT MARRIED "THE RIGHT WAY"

Upon completion of one interview I remember a particular spouse saying "Those questions aren't exactly what I had expected." I told her that they weren't especially "academic sounding" questions but were born rather out of all the questions that I had had over my lifetime as a spouse. The interview questions were birthed out of my perceptions of what I believed was happening inside of Super Couple marriages. Besides questions on the demographic makeup of this population, two of my very first questions "How did you meet?" and "Did you ever have any other long-term relationships or previous marriages?" were based on my first erroneous assumption that Super Couples did everything "the right way." Let me tell you what I mean by that.

Because my marriage had so many initial difficulties I attributed them to the fact that I had messed things up by not getting married the traditional way. I erroneously assumed that Super Couples fell into that population that also did things "the right way." I got pregnant at a young age, married my boyfriend, *then* had a wedding a year later on our first anniversary, and almost twenty years later earned my first college degree. I used to tell my daughters "I don't care how old you are when you marry, just do it the right way: get your degree, get engaged, get married, and only then have a kid or two, you know...the opposite of me. I was certain, too, that most Super Couples were on their first marriages because after all, data have shown that second marriages have a higher failure rate than first marriages. While this statistic is absolutely correct, I began to learn that though most Super Couples were on their first marriages (75%), that the 25% on their second or third marriages (and equally as

Super) definitely did *not* do things the traditional way either. One of my most loving Super Couples was the product of an affair. Again, while most second marriages and those that result from an affair go on to have the same struggles as the couples' first marriages, (and fail at an even higher rate) this research shows that that does not have to be the case. (It should be noted though that nearly all affairs end—and end painfully— especially marriages that were the product of an affair.) Each of these couples often became Super not because they picked a different spouse, but precisely because they began to *do* things differently in their second marriages than they did in their first. They *chose* to learn from their mistakes and change their *own* attitudes and behaviors. So while most Super Couples did do things "the right way" this was not an essential part of the Super Couple formula.

I know with certainty that I am not alone in this erroneous assumption that there is a right way and a wrong way to come together because to one degree or another nearly every couple that speaks to me about their troubled marriages says something similar to this statement "Well, if only we'd have dated longer" or "I think we just dated for too long before we got married and we just felt everyone *expected* us to marry" or "We figured it was the next logical step, though we really should not have married at all." One couple I met with just this week began by saying "I am forty nine and she is forty one. I guess our difference in age has finally caught up with us." Seriously? You're only eight years apart, not thirty years. Some couples claim they were simply too young and immature in their early twenties or late teens to have gotten married while still others claim they were too old at forty-something (usually they blame their spouse for having been too old and "set in his/ her ways" to have made the marriage work). Do you see where I am going with this? No matter what our initial situation, once the painful or work-required years arrive, we all begin to look backwards to justify why we believe we need to get out of our marriages. The human heart is so tender it will do anything in its power to make hurt and pain go away. Likewise, the human brain is brilliant and can rationalize any set of circumstances whatsoever to accommodate one's current marital situation—

especially when well-meaning friends and the media help us to do so.

It makes sense that couples look backwards into the microscope of their relational history to figure out where they went wrong. We retrace the steps that could lead to clarity and answers regarding the causes of our troubled marriages. *Was it me? Was it my spouse? What could I have done differently?* Of course, hindsight is 20/20. But the problem for so many is a misappropriation of responsibility onto static factors that absolve *us* of fault such as our age, years together, or circumstances: *He was a spender. I was a saver. It could not have worked.* As this research found, there was no one right way for the couples' unions. Each came together based on a unique set of circumstances.

No matter what the perceived reason for the hurt, pain, or trouble in one's marriage, most everyone claims it failed because of having not gotten married the "right" way, claiming for the most part the marriage was doomed from the beginning. So let me say this clearly right here: **There is no right way**!

That being said, I urge you to get to know your future spouse as best as possible before you marry in order to establish a strong and intimate friendship before you say "I do" (one of the strongest elements in Super Couple marriages). That is definitely an *easier way* to minimize the future potential of difficulties that often lead to divorce. But I am also the same person who will tell you that marriages do not fail based on the circumstances of how you came together *before* marriage either, i.e. "We never really knew each other well enough." Marriages fail because of the choices we make *within* our marriages. Those choices of what to say and do (or not do) to and with your spouse will determine the demise or success of your marriage. Consider arranged marriages. Studies have shown that arranged marriages are more fulfilling than non-arranged marriages (Bentley, 2011) and according to a study by Barker (2011), love in arranged marriages is twice that reported in "love" or non-arranged marriages. While the thought of an arranged marriage might seem ridiculous and incomprehensible to most Westerners, the point still stands that the "how" of a couple's coming together is significantly less important than what takes place within the marriage. So to be clear, there are paths that make the potential of attaining "Super" a bit easier than others, but none are ever truly the reasons for marital Superness or demise.

FAULTY ASSUMPTION 2:
THEY LEARNED "SUPER" FROM THEIR PARENTS

Next, based on data that imply we are greatly influenced by our families of origin, my second faulty assumption about what caused Superness inspired me to ask about the marriages of the parents of our Super spouses. "Were your parents married or not? Happy or not?" I sought to discover whether or not Super Couples were Super because they *learned* to be Super from their parents. The responses to this question revealed that while many of the Super Spouses interviewed were children of parents whose marriages often lasted until death, most of those were simply due to the generational differences regarding marriage and divorce. Their parents married during a time when commitment was epic and divorce not an option. Period. As such, though many of their parents had sustained marriages, none of them were believed by their children to have had *Super* marriages. Brooke had never heard her father say "I love you," Gina came from an alcoholic father who was an angry man to his wife. Jenny's father was a philanderer. She absolutely did not want that repeated in her own marriage. Maggie's father, too, was extremely unfaithful and produced 50+ siblings by numerous other women! Larry's mom was bipolar and "evil." Troy's mother was bitter and controlling. To sum it up, almost all of these couples were raised by parents that were either divorced or definitely in unhappy marriages. So apparently *that* wasn't the secret.

Our families of origin clearly influence us, our personalities, and our decisions well into adulthood and beyond. But when it came to the *extreme happiness* or Superness of these couples, their parents' influence seemed to be no more an accurate predictor than were their decisions to do things "the right way" either. In actuality, if my analysis were to show any correlations between families of origin and Super marriages it would be that Super Couples often became Super because they learned precisely what *not* to do from their parents. Larry had a mean and schizophrenic, and "evil incarnate" mother that would call him names like idiot and fatty. After recalling the hurtfulness he said *"you don't call somebody that you deeply love an idiot and you're supposed to deeply love your spouse and your children."* When asked if he made a conscious decision never to call his wife or children hurtful names he said, *"No I never made a decision, I just don't do it."* Though Larry states that his decision to be different than his mother was not a conscious one, his recollection shows that at least on a subconscious level Larry made a choice to do the opposite of what his parents did. Maggie and Jenny did the same. Their fathers were philanderers so they knew what they did not want and took steps to best ensure they did not repeat those patterns. Though each of these couples made a conscious or subconscious choice in their mate selection based on the poor marital examples their parents set, what is now known is that family of origin is not a necessary factor to marital Superness.

FAULTY ASSUMPTION 3:
THEY NEVER ENDURED ANY MAJOR STRUGGLES

A third assumption I had regarding the Superness of these couples was that they must have never endured any *major* difficulties or hardships. I asked if they had, and if those struggles were major or minor. After all, if they had fewer struggles than most they'd have little to fight about, right? As I already pointed out, these couples dealt with some pretty major issues. One wife had a nervous breakdown, Larry's bipolar mother moved in with them at the onset of their marriage and tried to break them up. So, my assumption was again proven inaccurate and thus my curiosity even more piqued as to what these couples had that the rest of us did not.

Additionally, when we ask about big or little struggles, what was also learned is that for Super Couples, all struggles are minimized by the ways in which they respectfully deal with those struggles and that paradoxically, unhappy couples' troubles were made to appear large or insurmountable precisely *because of* the poor ways they dealt with them. While I believed my husband

and I dealt with conflicts and troubles of great magnitude (as measured by my degree of hurt and desire to escape the painful situations), through a backward glance it becomes apparent that the difficulties we, like many other hurting couples, endured were not that insurmountable at all but rather small. Though we rarely had enough money for our wants, we always found money for our needs. We never worried about food or shelter, our children were not sick or on drugs, they *thrived* in school, we went to church weekly, had family meals, and years later, both of our daughters married good, loving, and God-fearing men. What difficulties were so insurmountable that we were miserable and caused me to contemplate divorce? So while we will deal with this more fully in the chapter on conflict, it is important to state here that it's not the size of marriage difficulties that matter but "how" they are managed that facilitates a super or not-so-super marriage.

FAULTY ASSUMPTION 4:
THEY WERE NEVER ATTRACTED TO OTHERS BESIDES THEIR SPOUSE

This fourth and extremely inaccurate assumption about the Super Couple secret circled around the idea of romantic attraction. In my ignorance I used to believe that if you really loved someone that you'd stop being attracted to other people. Stop laughing at me! Cut me some slack as there is a kernel of truth in this hugely faulty assumption. But as I aged, I discovered that just because one was married didn't mean he or she stopped being attractive or attracted to others. Actually, the very opposite can easily take place, as human nature dictates that we often want that which we cannot have.

"You can eat any of these seven hundred and eighty-five varieties of desserts...but you cannot have any pecan pie."

"Wait. What? Why can't I have pecan pie? What's wrong with pecan pie? I mean, look at those pecans...freshly roasted, oh so tantalizing...and the *smell*. That pie smells awesome!"

"There is absolutely nothing wrong with pecan pie but it wouldn't be good for you. It's no big deal though. Look at the giant, delectable, double-layered piece of *Death by Chocolate* you have in front of you. You should be so happy to have that slice of cake. Everyone else envies you having gotten this slice. It's the best dessert on the menu."

"Yeah, I know. I love *Death by Chocolate* but I've had it every night for the past three years. I am really admiring that pecan pie over there. What kind of pecans did you put in it anyway? Did you roast them in butter first? Wow, they really smell great."

"Well, yes we did, but don't worry about the pecan pie. Your doctor said you can't have any. It wouldn't really be good for you. Remember sir, you're allergic to pecans and I am fairly certain the resulting anaphylactic shock would not be worth the risk."

"Well, there is that. Then how about this lemon merengue?"

"Sir, you *hate* lemons! Have you forgotten your long ago comment that *Death by Chocolate* was by far the best dessert God ever created and you'd never love another dessert more?"

"I know. Fine. ...but about this pecan pie... It's just not fair. I really wish I could have some pecan pie..."

Ah, the forbidden fruit. Crazy isn't it? We can have the world and ninety percent of all that is in it, but our focus seems naturally to shift from what we have to what we do not have. Relationships are the same way. As soon as we marry we immediately, though very happy (ninety percent of the time), become aware of all the others we *cannot* have and those numerous off-limits others become even more attractive to us. The less relationally mature we are the less likely we are to recognize this inevitability and often find ourselves "looking at the harmless menus" again and pondering its forbidden fruit. Once this begins to take place, problems ensue. As a matter of fact, one wise Super Wife seemed to instinctively have learned of this problematic thinking (or became aware of it over the years as she journeyed toward Superness) that when the concept of "looking at the menu" was brought up she responded "Why should I look at the menu if I know I can't order? Why would I want to tease myself like that? And what if I found something on the menu that *looked* more appealing to me than what I had already ordered? Then what are my options? To leave my husband with whom I've already begun to build a life only to go onto an unknown that only *appears* to be better? What a predicament that would be. No, thank you. I will keep my eyes focused on my own menu." How wise she was.

Many of my other Super Spouses implied or directly said similar things. But they all defaulted to "I *choose* to keep my eyes on my spouse." They chose to maintain solid boundaries around their eyes and their hearts to protect their marriages because of their keen awareness of the dangers of attractiveness to and for another human being—both physical and emotional attractiveness.

So again, in my idyllic search for the Super Couple formula my mind would subconsciously elevate Super Spouses to a level that would have them immune to this unfortunate (?) fact of life that we do not stop being attracted or attractive to others. I believed that once they found their "Super Spouse" they no longer had to deal with the temptation of loving another because, after all, they had a Super Spouse. In an attempt to defend my youthful ignorance I must remind you that this idea was based in part on what actually takes place in the initial stages of nearly every romantic relationship. While this will be developed more fully later in the book when we discuss the brain changes and "the love cocktail" (Gottman), when we first fall in love with our future spouse we are so hyper-focused on this person that nearly nothing or no one else is able to divert or capture our attention. As one friend of mine always jokes "someone could walk past my husband with her hair on fire and he wouldn't notice." While she was not serious (I hope) about her husband's true response, the idea is the same: when we are so transfixed by someone or something, nothing else will be able to capture our attention or turn that focus.

If we want to take this argument a step further it could be claimed that happily married men and women actually become *more* attractive to others precisely because of the attractive nature of Superness. Movies like *The Notebook* are successful because its viewers are attracted to "a love like theirs" and thus "a man like that" or "a woman like her." Because we often find those love stories attractive, we likewise find those lovers attractive. Super Spouses become more attractive to others because of their observed ability to love. I've witnessed this quite often in my lifetime and as a researcher. Women, more so than men, find a man more attractive who loves his wife. Oh, the irony.

So my initial idea wasn't exactly alien to rational thinking:

if I really love my spouse then few others will be as attractive to me as is my spouse. While I will fully develop this idea in our chapter on redefining *love,* I will point out that the actions involved in falling in love are also the same actions required to remain in love with *and attracted to* that person. If those same actions are directed toward a new person, they will arouse an attraction to that person as well. And that's a big problem.

FAULTY ASSUMPTION 5:
THEY COULDN'T POSSIBLY BE MARRIED TO PESSIMISTS

Pessimists are hard to take—especially if one is an optimist. They can be toxic as they tend to see problems before ever seeing good, or they see no good at all. "You'd better not try that business venture. You know how many businesses fail? You've got no business experience at all. You'd better wait until...No, no. I believe in you...but..." If you're married to this person this poses a bigger problem: I can either run from you to stop your toxicity from snuffing out my joy and positivity or I can surrender and allow your misery to cover my life as well. Unfortunately, neither option is ideal.

Because Super Couples are extraordinary in their love for one another, appear to always be happy with one another, and never complain about their spouse outside of the privacy of their own environment (because true Super Couples have learned to keep their constructive criticisms of one another contained within the privacy of their own conversations with one another), it could be assumed, as I did, that Super Couples cannot be both Super and pessimistic. The two simply can't seem to coexist.

Optimists are the opposite. They tend to see all that is good and right with the world. Optimists tend to see good and positive outcomes in people, places, and situations where others might have to squint to do so. So while I expected to find that all my Super Couples were optimists married to optimists I was surprised to discover they were not. A good percentage of my couples usually had at least one person who characterized him or herself as an optimist while their spouses characterized themselves as leaning toward pessimism or, as they called it, realism. Hmm...yet again I was seeing something I had not expected to see: one's optimistic or pessimistic perspective had little to do with the Superness of one's marriage. To my credit, I did discover I wasn't fully off track in my assumption. I simply mislabeled what I perceived to be problematic as pessimism. After a longer series of interviews I realized it wasn't pessimism or optimism that influenced Superness but rather a trait that should not have surprised me at all, for it was the very same trait that all centenarians shared (people who live to be one hundred years old or older), the same trait found in great leaders, and the same trait found in the motivators and inspirational leaders of the world. What I was really recognizing was a couple's degree of *encouragement* versus *discouragement* of one another in their interactions. That all Super Spouses were exceptionally encouraging of their mates began to become increasingly apparent through each subsequent interview. My Super Couples exemplified encouragement—richly.

Many of us are familiar with the phrase "One can move mountains if he/she has enough faith." Whether or not we accept the Judeo-Christian ideology from where this phrase originated, it is fair to say that we much more easily see the power *others* have to move the mountain than we do in ourselves. We are our own worst critics, no matter who we are or what we may try to say on the outside. I know me. I know my flaws, my weaknesses, and my failings, so when you try to tell me about something you think I can do or something I am good at it is easy for me to discount it or simply take what you say with a grain of salt. "Thank you Sara for complimenting my recent seminar." (But in my head I immediately discount it because "she has no idea that I totally missed one of my important pieces of information and was talking too fast from nerves." I can't *really* expect to ever get hired as a full-time trainer because I'm just so average.")

Paradoxically, it is precisely because many of us have such a keen awareness of so many of our flaws and failings that we do not need you to point them out to us and make us focus on them even more. I need you to build me up, not tear me down, to tell me where I am strong, not where I am weak. Of course there are some flaws that cannot and must not be overlooked, like one who has an addiction and is blind to it but, for the most part we are speaking of non-detrimental, basic personality flaws and human failings that one can live with perpetually but would do good to minimize proportionately with age and wisdom. For many years, and because I witnessed this in my own marriage, I believed the above example and others like it were a result of the differences between an optimistic and a pessimistic outlook. But I was mistaken. Once it was made obvious to me that I was looking at the encouragement/discouragement dichotomy, the faultiness of my assumption that pessimists could not be both married to an optimist *and* be Super made perfect sense. While there is more about encouragement in Part Three when the *Super Couple* formula is developed, rest assured that optimists and pessimists actually can live happily ever after.

FAULTY ASSUMPTION 6:
THEY WERE MORE ALIKE THAN DIFFERENT

When I set out to discover the "Super Couple Formula" years ago, and while my marriage was still deeply troubled, I thought there had to be something more specific and identifiable in the personalities of these individuals. They just had to be more alike than different. Right? Most specifically, I felt they had to have the same or similar temperaments. I mean when these couples "got lucky" in love, it must have been because they did a better job than I did at choosing mates whose personalities were more in sync with or similar to their own. For instance, clearly, Super Couples must either both be extraverts or both introverts in order to be extremely happy together. Right? Now to be clear, I knew numerous couples who had had long-term marriages and one was an extravert and the other an introvert. That wasn't my concern. Those marriages were just *average* marriages based on my perception. They did not stand out in the crowd as do Super Couples. They were likely content or even happy, but clearly they were not *extremely* happy—remember, these were my perceptions but not necessarily accurate or true.

I wanted to be Super and since I felt that because my husband and I were opposites—one extravert and one introvert—that Super would simply, yet again, never be possible for us. As such, for many years I had wished my husband was an extravert like me. That way we'd actually have some fun together doing the same activities. But noooo...my husband had to be a boring introvert who only enjoyed doing things alone like working on cars, or gardening or, worse yet, hunting! Why couldn't he be a fun spouse like me who enjoyed parties, amusement parks, dancing, and any other activity that involved fifty or more of our closest friends? Why did he have to be so rude around other people and not be "the life of the party" like me?

I truly was ignorant of relationships to a greater degree early in my marriage than one expects to be in her youth. Most all of us are. And though, as I've already stated, I am not proud of my previous ignorance and resultant perspectives toward my husband, I am also quite cognizant of the fact that I am not alone and that many of you might also share similar perspectives—that people have to be the same or similar in their love languages, the same or similar in their likes and dislikes, the same or similar in their temperaments and personalities in order to have happy, long-term and thriving marriages. I know this because over the years I've been asked at least a thousand times by couples if they married the wrong person because their personalities or love languages were so radically dissimilar. After I delivered a temperament seminar many years ago, an adult male in his thirties (married for over ten years at that point) came to me with the printout of his personality type as well as his wife's and said "Should we be together or divorced." *And he was serious.* My prior ignorance was validated.

Just this week, a woman and very close friend to me articulated these very same errant sentiments as she and her husband began a period of marital separation. A second woman who is sadly filing for divorce said to me, her husband is unwilling to work at the marriage because he believes "we are simply too different" and therefore not meant for one another. One of these women was in her twenties and the other in her late forties. It seems this errant assumption is not mine alone but deeply embedded into our collective cultural psyches. I was greatly saddened by both these women's statements because they are absolutely untrue as the source of their marital demises. I also now know that being different or even on completely opposite ends of the personality spectrum are not only *not* the source of marital dissatisfaction but rather the converse is true:

Super Couples are actually more different than alike in many of these areas.

Most of our likes and dislikes, hobbies and professions are chosen because they "fit" well with our personalities. Thus when most couples assert that they are too "different" to be happy, they are often referring primarily to their differences in introversion or extraversion because these differences greatly direct our preferences for particular hobbies, careers, and social environments. As such, a focus on extraversion and introversion will help us to understand most other "differences" couples experience while striving for marital happiness.

Both of the women above who stated that they were so different from their spouses I know to be strong introverts. Their husbands are both strong extraverts. I get this. It's the same world in which I've been living for more than three decades, just reversed.

For the past two decades I have been enamored with Temperament theory. Temperament theory goes all the way back to approximately 450 BC when Hippocrates determined that there were four basic temperaments. That is, of all people ever born, in any nation and from any period of history that all people in the world would fall into one of four basic temperaments based on their first and foremost natural way of responding to the world. For example, most of us are right-handed though some of us are left-handed. Neither is right nor wrong, good nor bad. It is just that one hand is more comfortable or *preferred* by its user than the other. It is the same with our preferences for extroverting or introverting ourselves as well. There is nothing *wrong* with either. We simply all have a preference for one or the other. Additionally, while there are numerous temperament models in existence today (Kiersey-Bates, DISC, The Four Lenses, Meyers-Briggs [the one I prefer to use], etc.), nearly all of them break human personalities into four different groups.

While the focus of this book is not on personalities, I recommend everyone seek to learn basic temperament theory, since understanding personality differences is beneficial to the argument of marital Superness. Too many people like me, have, in times of marital trouble, defaulted to the erroneous belief that only certain personality types are meant to be together or can ever make it to Super. If you are interested in learning more about temperament there are literally hundreds of books available to help you understand yourself and your mate better. It helps you to "cut them mental slack" as I often tell my seminar participants. As a matter of fact, if your relationship is struggling it might be precisely *because* one of you is ignorant of human behaviors and personalities. Become an expert in your mate and happiness *will* follow.

The MBTI model explains personality preferences through four different dichotomies. Each dichotomy represents a different aspect of our personalities: Extraversion versus Introversion seeks to explain from where we get our energy; Sensing versus Intuition seeks to explain how we take in information; Thinking versus Feeling seeks to explain how we prefer to make decisions; and lastly Judging versus Perceiving seeks to explain our outer world orientation—do we prefer more closure or more options? Based on these four dichotomies MBTI mathematically breaks personalities into sixteen different types (I'm an ESFJ—the hosts and hostesses of the world). As stated earlier, the focus here will be on one dichotomy: extraversion versus introversion. Not only is this the most easily understood of the four, but it is also the most often discussed in terms of a couple's initial attraction to one another, their subsequent long-term relationship and, most importantly, often the most problematic in terms of presenting problems of the marital relationship.

I am an off-the-charts extrovert. My husband (because God clearly has a sense of humor) is an off-the-charts introvert. Unlike what most commonly believe, this dichotomy is not about being shy or outgoing (though there are definite correlations between the two) but rather it explains from where we get our energy. Let me begin with extraverts. Extraverts get their actual physiological energy from the outer world: from people, places, and events. As such, we gain energy by going to malls, parties, and sporting events where many other people are. We prefer running clubs and working out in group classes because the energy alone is enough to motivate us further than when we work out alone. We choose for hobbies activities that keep us around groups of people like book clubs, drama clubs, knitting clubs, etc. Depending on the degree of extraversion, we might nearly always choose the group setting for our activities and employment over the individual or private setting. Over my lifetime I realized that I was always happiest when I worked at the busy, people-filled main offices in the biggest parts of the city. Working in the small satellite offices simply bored me, as I didn't have enough daily interaction with my energy source: people. Don't get me wrong; I loved my cubicle and my cave time. I just needed significantly less of it than did my introverted colleagues. As such, I'd often take a break from my cave time to go gain a little energy extroverting with a colleague...then, when my energy tank was filled, I'd get back to work with renewed energy—and work twice as fast with twice the focus than before I extroverted myself.

As an extravert, I've taught seminars to groups as small as five people and while I'm certain I'm still brilliant in my delivery (ha ha), I am much less energized than when I teach seminars to audiences of fifty, five hundred, or even thousands of people. When I finish those seminars I have so much resultant energy I can go for a ten-mile jog afterwards, can clean my entire house like a maid on steroids, and can talk at the pace of a keyboard gone mad for the next hour or so...or until my energy source is removed for a sufficient period of time. When a strong extravert is around large groups of people it is as if they have been plugged into an electrical outlet and can keep on moving until their energy source is removed, such as once they are alone or in a small group for an extended period of time. (Side note: If you want your extraverted children to go to sleep quickly, separate them from the others and give them alone time. Soon that child will be yawning and found asleep with an open book resting near her fingertips. Put this child in a room with siblings and it will seem like an endless number of "Quiet down in there!" shouts will be necessary to get the talking and giggling to cease and desist).

Additionally, people who prefer extraversion tend *to extravert* (the verb) their thoughts through either the spoken or the written word. They must speak-to-think. (My poor husband. I know. Please send your contributions to the Danny Bacon Ear Plug Fund for Sanity.) So when there exists an issue or a concern, an extravert will be the first one to begin talking about it. Talking things out (even when there is no issue but rather just thoughts on an interesting topic) helps extraverts to process their thoughts and feelings. After going on and on about a certain topic my husband will often say, "What on earth are you trying to say?" to which I respond, "I don't know yet. Disregard seventy-five percent of what I'm saying. When I am finished I will know." All you extraverts out there are now saying "Amen sister!" and high-fiving each other "So that's what I've been doing all of these years!" For extraverts talking *is* the filter through which we parse our thoughts—which is why many of us extraverts have foot-in-mouth disease, like me...and I have a size nine and a half mouth to prove it.

Introverts are just the opposite. Introverts get their energy from the inner world of thoughts, ideas, and concepts. Those who prefer introversion are energized by their internal world where they have the time and space *to think* about those issues and topics important or intriguing to them without the distractions of the loud, outer world. The very things that tend to energize an extravert will just as often drain the introvert and vice versa. Introverts tend to work out on their own (they're the ones in the gym with headphones on to ward off any potential talkers), prefer hobbies that allow them to introvert such as gardening, reading, running (alone), painting (alone), etc. Actually, introverts and extraverts can share many of the same interests. It's just that for extraverts the word "club" will often follow: gardening club, reading club, running club, etc. And unlike extraverts, introverts often choose careers that will also satisfy their preference for staying in their inner world as much as possible. Unlike me, my husband totally prefers and thrives in the small satellite offices tucked far away from human civilization. While he's awesome and excels no matter where he is, when he works in small, intimate settings he thrives. This is, in part, the reason he also switched careers mid-life to the environmental field where he is daily required to go alone into "the field" for hours at a time. He drives alone. He walks the particular field or forest alone, and he writes his permits alone. He loves it. The quiet setting energizes him and brings him great joy.

However, when it comes to communication, the preference

for introversion or extraversion has little relationship at all to the *quality* of one's communication or relational skills but only the *location* of those communicative exchanges. The primary difference is related to *where* the processing takes place—inside or outside of one's head. I point this out because I've regularly heard others associate good public speaking skills to extraversion as if only extraverts can be great public speakers. This is absolutely untrue. The primary difference is that after the introvert delivers her brilliant seminar she is drained and needs to go to her cave or private space to recharge. The energy source or electrical outlet for the introvert is in the quiet, private space of her mind—uninterrupted by the outer world. For the time that she has been extroverting publicly that introvert has been spending her energy and will ultimately feel drained. When a strong introvert with high-quality communication skills *does speak* however, what usually comes out are extremely thoughtful and powerful words—few, but powerful—because they have been thoroughly parsed in the mind before exiting the lips.

Thoroughly...

for hours...

or days...

or weeks...

Some introverts are extremely content *never* extroverting a particular thought or situation, as after he or she has processed it internally it is finished, resolved, completed...for him or her at least.

Paradoxical to the extravert, when there is an issue, concern or intrigue, the introvert tends to prefer processing those thoughts internally before ever uttering the first word. More so, unless required to do so (based on a given situation or the needs of the other) those with a strong preference for introversion will often simply come to conclusions about issues or concerns without ever having externalized their thoughts once. And they move on. Their preference for introverting is often so strong that they clearly envision themselves talking to their mates (or with whomever they have an issue) and even envision themselves discussing the solution with the other person...without ever having uttered a word. I've seen *this* get a lot of introverts in trouble in their marriages.

Introvert: *"I already discussed this situation with you. Why can't you let it go?"*

Extravert: *"No you didn't. You haven't said a word to me about it since I brought it to your attention!"*

Introvert: *"I could have sworn we talked about it."*

Extravert: *"When? Where?"*

Introvert: *"Umm...well...I was pretty sure we did..."*

Having given this example in hundreds of seminars it usually garners a lot of chuckling and elbow-hitting from my Introvert/Extravert couples who look at each other and nod approvingly in admission that this scenario has often played out in their own relationships. It's always comical when discussed, but the truth of the matter is that knowledge is power. Once made aware of these tendencies, people can work with them and seek to improve in these areas. To reiterate, unlike extraverts who speak-to-think, introverts think-to-speak—or speak as infrequently as possible depending on the preferred degree of introversion. When these two get married, that's when the real "fun" begins. Speaking and thinking isn't the only area problematic differences manifest in these "mixed" marriages.

As mentioned earlier, the areas couples will most readily notice having clear manifestations of their differing temperaments is in their choices of hobbies, careers, or in their preference to reason through conflict externally (through either the written or spoken word) or internally (through their thoughts). However, there is another issue that is often judged even more problematic when an introvert marries an extravert.

Often, I have had a spouse come to me to help resolve for them the recurring issue of privacy. After years of answering this same question it now makes me internally smile each time the question is posed because I know that both spouses are standing there privately poised to hear my response as if in hopes of then turning to their spouse to say "See, I told you I was right."

Recently, one of my absolutely favorite Super Couples (because their communication seemed to be so in sync with one another) approached me with this question:

"Christine, several times when Jenny and I have had a discussion on a particular topic we will differ on whether or not this is a private conversation. One of us will often share parts of the conversation with others while the other considers it private."

Ah...spoken in true Super Couple fashion. The spouse posing the question, in this case Pete, would not reveal who held which opinion in order to protect that person should I have considered his or her opinion flawed. He didn't want Jenny to be hurt or even to be made to feel bad if I had chosen his side. That was very kind. It didn't matter though. I knew exactly who did what because I knew that Jenny was, like me, an off-the-charts extravert while Pete was an introvert. I told them that simply, privacy was little more than an extravert/introvert issue.

To greater or lesser degree, extraverts are publicly open while introverts are publicly guarded. As such, there is significantly less that extraverts consider private or off limits. There is very little I consider private (as you can tell by my numerous exposed secrets in this book). Most topics can be shared with *at least* one other close friend. Introverts are significantly more guarded in their communications and consider many more of their human experiences private than do their extraverted friends or spouses.

Facebook is a good example of our differing needs for privacy. I believe the last time I looked I had more than a thousand "friends." My thoughts are that I don't have much information on my page that I consider secret so what could it hurt to let them see the pictures of my perfect grandchildren or the post of my having done a mud run in North Carolina for instance. My sister, a strong introvert, has few Facebook friends. This is not because she is not a likeable person, because she is very well-liked. But I recall an example she shared with me one day that perfectly exemplifies this difference in privacy preferences. After dropping her kids off at school she met a few other mothers in the parking lot for the first time. They had a pleasant conversation and went their separate ways. When she returned home she noticed a Facebook "friend request" from one of the women she had just met. Her response to me was "Why on earth would I want to "friend" this person? I barely know her? I don't want her looking at my pictures and knowing about my private life." Yep, that's a true introvert. There is nothing wrong with her preference for privacy. It's simply *different* than mine.

While you can see it's no big deal to me that my sister and I tolerate different levels of privacy, it is often a source of great discomfort when these two are married to one another and one spouse shares information the other wishes to protect. I have joked with my husband, "Honey, it's okay if I tell them you have blue eyes. They can pretty much figure that out just by looking at you!"

To reiterate, being "different" from one's spouse is *not* the cause of marital breakdown. It's how we handle those differences that strengthens or weakens a marriage. In a later chapter we will address the true cause of marital erosion when it comes to appreciating or disparaging our differences.

Let me bring up one more consideration regarding similarities and differences. Social scientists have identified the Theory of Matching, which for the most part says people are more likely to form successful relationships with and express liking for people whose level of physical attractiveness roughly equals their own. I want to point out that this theory focuses on *physical* similarities for the most part: pretty people tend to marry pretty people. People who consider themselves of average attractiveness tend to marry others who are averagely attractive. In addition to physical similarities, we marry others whose values are most similar to ours: people with conservative values tend to marry others with conservative values; those with more liberal values marry others who, too, hold more liberal values. Atheists tend to marry other non-believers, Christians marry Christians, etc. No matter how much married couples might be struggling and focusing on their "differences" their most deeply-held values remain similar. However, Temperament research shows that we are attracted to and tend to marry those whose personality traits *oppose* ours. As a matter of fact, many introverts are attracted to extraverts (and vice versa) precisely because one prefers to talk more while the other prefers to listen. This works out quite well in many relationships—especially in the initial stages when we are trying to get to know one another better—as it is not usually *what* is said that hurts or helps relational communication but rather *how* one says what he or she says that truly makes the difference.

So while a misappropriation of the Theory of Matching (matching love languages, temperaments, hobbies) seems to poison the thoughts of many who believe Super Couples are Super because they are more alike, when it comes to our personalities, being "different" isn't the cause of our troubles. When marriages are troubled, blame shifts to the negative differences rather than the positive differences. So rest assured that while nearly all couples are most similar in their deeply-held values that infrequently, if ever, change, differences in personalities, however, are not the problematic culprits they are made out to be.

So that's it. I went into this research with several assumptions of what it was that created or hindered Superness and none were accurate. They had little to do with what it was that these couples truly did have that made their marriages Super. Rather than continue to focus on what does *not* make a Super Couple, we will now begin to focus on the things that actually do.

Part II:

WHAT I HEARD IN INTERVIEWS

"I WOULD *NEVER* WANT TO HURT MY SPOUSE!"
LOVE IS KIND...

I am always embarrassed at the things that now seem like common sense to me or that I refer to as my "no-duh" moments because at one point those same moments were so foreign to me that they should have stood out like a dairy cow in a ten-acre field of dandelions, but did not. The phrase "I would *never* want to hurt my spouse!" was one of them. How could that be? I'm a Ph.D. in marriage and hearing those words from one spouse of another *surprised me*. Shouldn't that have been obvious? Shouldn't that be the mantra of *every* married couple? Well, it certainly *should be,* but sadly it is not. I likely hurt my husband all the time. My callous words and frequent name-calling displayed anything but the desire not to hurt him but rather to tear him down, to hurt him right back when he said or did something first to hurt, irritate, or frustrate me.

But I must begin with the obvious. Because I am neither unintelligent nor ignorant, my first analysis begins with trying to understand what could have so easily blinded me—and quite possibly blinds you—to this truth. How did we miss this?

When you first started dating your spouse would you have wanted to hurt him or her? Never! If so, you know they would not have wanted a second date. We dated precisely *because* the opposite took place: you not only did not *want* to hurt your lover you did your best to *ensure* you did nothing that would produce any negative emotions whatsoever. While dating, most of us did the opposite, and did everything in our power to produce feelings of happiness, peace, and contentment within our lovers.

If your date expressed embarrassment that he hadn't had enough time to shave for the date you'd have likely minimized that embarrassment by saying, "It's okay, I like that scruffy look." Or if they expressed dissatisfaction with their inability to have moved up in ranks at their jobs, we'd have likely shared a sentiment that lets them know we understand their dissatisfaction but would never have tried to hurt them with that information with a comment such as "Geez, what's wrong with you? Are you lacking in ambition?" Of course not. Just writing that seems laughable. Yet, embarrassingly, many couples do, in fact, hurt their spouses with words or actions. Why is this even a topic for discussion? Because it happens so frequently. The reasons will be dealt with in our chapter on trust. For now know that with Super Couples, the idea of hurting one's spouse is incomprehensible.

At some point in my interviews, my Super Spouses would express deliberateness in making sure they never do or say anything hurtful to their spouse. There is a kindness and thoughtfulness in the ways in which they spoke to one another. This is not to say that during interviews Super Spouses always agreed with one another. In fact, I can't remember a single interview where we didn't touch on points of disagreement. This happened all the time—as it does in any marriage. But when these areas of disagreement became manifest in our conversations, my Super Spouses seemed to tread even more softly than in their areas of agreement. They chose words that were soft, kind and non-judgmental. More so, Super Spouses would find ways to allow the other to express their differences and then seek an opportunity to validate their spouse's perception. In one such instance, Gina and Duane had just discussed her perception that he was a pessimist while she was an optimist. While Duane didn't initially hold this same perception (he felt he was a realist of course), his beautiful bride found a way to phrase it back in a way that actually complimented Duane for this personality trait. "Well, you do have a way of grounding me and helping me to see those things I might not have considered." Of course Duane was still not fully satisfied with this new knowledge of Gina's perception, but true to Super Couple form of not wanting to discuss anything potentially perceived as negative about his spouse publicly (in this case me and my digital recorder) Duane told Gina "I'm intrigued by this perception and I can see we're going to have fun finishing this conversation later." Like all my Super Couples, neither spouse would ever say anything that might have potential for hurting the other.

I remember one interview when I posed the question I pose to every Super Couple "Did you ever get hurt, angry, or upset at or with your spouse?" Both, like all interviewees, answered that of course they did. "Who doesn't? We're only human you know." However, when focusing on the potential for inflicting hurt on one another the wife was instantly taken aback. Brooke actually gasped and teared up at the thought of hurting her husband, conveying to me that doing so would be equally as painful to her. I remember this moment touching me deeply—and humbling me—as I had often said hurtful words to my husband both intentionally and unintentionally. I felt deeply ashamed. Why was this idea so foreign to me? I vowed that moment to consciously attempt to never again hurt this man whom I had promised to love, honor, and cherish. What about you? Have you ever hurt your spouse? Was it unintentional? Or worse, have you done so deliberately? Regardless of what you *have done or said* in your marriage, know that if you are striving toward Super you must with great diligence seek to never again hurt your spouse either. Trust me. I sympathize with you because most of us hurt others when we first feel hurt *by them.*

For those of us who have admitted to ourselves that we have, in fact, hurt our spouses it's worthwhile to consider the transition from that time when we began dating (and hurting them was unconscionable) to the time when it became commonplace and unrecognizable. For me, I can still recall the first time my future husband hurt me. It likely stood out to me because prior to that hurtful encounter he had only made me feel loved and happy—like his princess.

I was only eighteen and he twenty and he was teaching me how to drive a stick shift. When my young, future husband met me he was driving a 1979 cherry blossom red, Pontiac Trans-Am—and he loved it. I guess I should have known he was head-over-heels for me when he allowed me to within a fifty-foot radius of his beloved piece of mechanical heaven. But he did. And to think he was also willing to allow me behind its wheel to teach me to drive it should have been recognized as a relative marriage proposal in itself. Actually, he was teaching all of my girlfriends how to drive stick that day. What a stud. When I eventually got my turn behind the wheel I was a natural. I had observed three other girlfriends being instructed, so that by my turn I knew exactly what I was to do. I got her in first gear and then second almost effortlessly. Danny complimented me right then and there. "Wow, you're good at this." I blushed. Unfortunately, I tend to overthink things. By my third or fourth try I began to overthink and lost the natural ability of my first attempts. During one such gear change I ground the gears loudly producing that all-too-familiar sound of metal grinding metal at which point my sweet boyfriend loudly yelled at me "Hey, watch it! What's wrong with you?" I was deeply hurt. He had never before spoken to me like that and at that moment I was treated as less important than his precious car. I got out right there in the middle of the road trying to hold back my tears (I failed) and refused to go any further. I told him to park his own car.

I don't know if he knew how hurt I was. Likely he did, as my reactions left little doubt. But here it is, thirty-plus years later and though he probably forgot about that interchange an hour later, I still remember it vividly. Oh, I know it's no big deal at this point and we obviously got over it but it was, in fact, a hurt. My boyfriend hurt me, albeit unintentionally. The problem is that we often store those hurts in our hearts and minds and, further, when opportunity presents itself, we are less diligent about holding back our own hurtful words, thereby beginning a negative pattern of hurting one another. The true significance of this problem is my having remembered this incident at all.

In every Super Couple interview when asked if they'd ever experienced any marital difficulties with one another, every Super Spouse immediately said "yes." They seemed to laugh at the question. However, when asked to share those difficulties every single spouse struggled to come up with an example. Eventually, they'd recall some long ago example that clearly had no residual negative effects on the couple. Why was this so? It was so because one of the strategies that fosters Superness is the ability to let go of hurts quickly so as not to be able to easily recall them in future disagreements. The fact that I still remember the incident three decades later showed that I, like numerous other couples, had stored it for later recall. This happens for various reasons. Many spouses do this to have ammunition for their next argument. Not always though. Some simply have extremely good emotional memories—good or bad. Regardless, we must recognize that our imperfect spouses will sometimes hurt us—much of the time it's unintentional. To hurt our spouses unintentionally, as I am certain my boyfriend did, is harmful to the relationship but can be, if infrequent, manageable. But to hurt our spouses intentionally is an altogether much more detrimental and insensitive act of carelessness. I am not sure of the first time that I hurt him, but I am certain that it became much more frequent over the years. We hurt because we were once hurt too. Yet, at some point it becomes less important to know who was the first than to recognize the pattern of hurting.

To be a Super Couple this pattern must stop. You cannot be Super in your love for your spouse if you are careless about your ability to inflict hurt on that person. More so, if you are not yet married I implore you to recognize that it is much easier to *prevent* this from ever becoming a pattern at the onset than to fix after it's become habit. Take it from one who knows. After decades of hurtful word choices it took much focused effort to undo the damage we had inflicted upon one another. However, the good news is that change is absolutely possible. My husband and I are now much more thoughtful about our word choices with one another than ever before. And why shouldn't we be? After all, as I strive to become a Super Wife, why would I ever want to hurt my spouse? What outcome would it produce but a negative one? Thus, measure your every utterance with utmost care and choose only the most tender words to express your thoughts and feelings. As you do, you will soon be on your way to Super. But kindness and "I would never want to hurt my spouse!" are only the first steps. The next stop: adoration.

I ADORE MY SPOUSE!

As mentioned earlier, "I adore my spouse!" was a phrase uttered by nearly every Super Wife interviewed. But what does this mean? Is it just a random and meaningless verb added to their vernacular to color their sentences, as has the word *awesome* become in our daily communications? Possibly, but it's doubtful because few other wives, apart from these extremely happy wives, seem to offer the same sentiments about their husbands. The dictionary definition of "adore" means to regard another person with the utmost esteem, love, and respect. It means to honor someone. While I'm certain few, if any, of my Super Spouses looked up the definition of adoring before they attached the verb to their spouse, it had become unquestionable through Super Couple interviews that *adoration* was exactly what was taking place. In order to better understand what these women meant by their statements of adoration it is essential to dig more deeply into the concepts to which adoration refers. As such, we will begin by breaking down more fully these concepts of honor, esteem, and respect. The final concept—love—will be afforded, necessarily, the greatest amount of discussion only afterwards for reasons both obvious and not so obvious.

HONOR

The dictionary lists numerous definitions of honor beginning with the nouns: honesty, fairness, or integrity in one's beliefs and actions: *a man of honor*; a source of credit or distinction: *to be an honor to one's family*; high respect, as for worth, merit, or rank: *to be held in honor*; such respect manifested: *a memorial in honor of the dead*; high public esteem; fame; glory: *He has earned his position of honor*. And it has equally as many definitions for the verb *to honor*: to hold in honor or high respect; revere: *to honor one's parents*; to treat with honor; to confer honor or distinction upon: *The university honored him with its leadership award*; to worship (the Supreme Being); to show a courteous regard for: *to honor an invitation*.

While not all of these definitions relate to the institution of marriage, it is important to list them to realize the power behind the words and commitments we've made but have long since forgotten. And if we've forgotten the meanings of the words we speak and the promises we've made, we are also ill-equipped to comprehend their importance in our lives and, most especially, in our marriages.

At one point, the promises *to love* and *to honor* were common marriage vows. However, at some point (and likely aided by the modern trend of couples writing their own vows), more and more couples have opted to take those words out of their marital vows. Was this out of ignorance of word meanings borne out of our attempts to modernize our promises? Or, worse yet, was this borne out of an actual *choice* to *not honor* our spouses at all? I'd like to believe it was the former: we just didn't think about the words *to honor*. But what if I am wrong? What if we've taken those words out of our vows by choice? *"I don't want to promise to honor my spouse because what if he/she doesn't deserve to be honored?"*

To hold in honor or high respect for another person—to revere that person—is a choice. Many would argue that some of these need to be earned before they are freely given. And that may be true. But if you consider how many individuals we honor or revere before we know much substantive information about them, it would be clear that honor is readily distributed in our society like penny candy in a confectionary. We honor donors who give large sums of money at our universities by naming buildings after them. I've been to numerous political events where guests pay thousands of dollars just to stand in line to shake hands and have their pictures taken with the guests of honor. And for what are they being honored? They are being honored and revered for simply holding a particular position as an elected official... or for simply *campaigning* to be one. That's it. While I'd like to believe most of those in office were elected for their honesty, fairness, and integrity in their beliefs and actions, much of the time they were elected because they had a larger sum of money to purchase political ads. Now they may, in fact, have those honorable characteristics, but the average populace has no idea of the accuracy of that belief. Thus, while these people may, in fact, be worthy of the honor of which they are being bestowed, those honoring them know little about whether or not the honor is "deserved." Consider the many congressman and senators who have had to resign their posts in shame after having done immoral or illicit things in their private lives—dishonoring themselves and the offices they held.

So honoring another is a choice. We decide to whom we wish

to extend it and we decide whether or not we wish to rescind it. In the case of the dishonorable public official, we will often rescind our honor after they've done something dishonorable. Fair enough. But are there positions and people that should always be held in honor or esteem regardless of the mistakes they've made? Or, in other words, should honor only be conferred upon those who have never made a mistake? If that is true, who could cast the first stone? There'd be plenty of honors with no one upon whom to confer them. I certainly would not be able to earn it or maintain it. So what does that mean? Should honor and reverence be a gift freely given out of love or respect? Should it only be given when the honoree is making no mistakes or bad decisions? What if ninety-eight percent of her decisions are honorable but two percent are not? Should we then still honor her? What if half of her decisions are honorable or only ten percent of them? Where do we draw the line?

So let's consider our spouses. When we fell in love with them, chances are we honored and revered them greatly, totally ignoring or disregarding any or most of their flaws or failings we may have been exposed to at that point. We were aware of many of the good things they had done up to that point (or at least based on the little that we knew) and whatever little it was we already knew of them, it was sufficient enough for them to receive our utmost honor...willingly and unquestionably. So, do you hold in honor or high respect *your spouse*—do you revere him/her? Or have you chosen to stop?

We likely have conferred great honor on our spouses at some point in our dating lives. Whether we once honored them and then chose to stop or we never built a strong enough foundation to have done so initially is less important than recognizing that Super Wives simply adore their husbands (I've not heard the husbands use the same phraseology) and that we should, if we seek to become Super Couples, consider seriously what this would look like in our own relationships. What might it look like if we did adore our spouses? And why do we not now adore them?

ESTEEM

It is a fair assumption that most individuals, families, and societies today are confused as to what or whom to esteem. I would guess many aren't sure what esteem is in the first place. The dictionary gives several definitions. And for the sake of applying esteem to our intimate relationships it becomes obvious all of them are relevant to those characteristics found in Super Couples. Beginning with the verbs, esteem is defined as "to regard highly or favorably" and "to regard with respect or admiration." As a noun, esteem is defined as "a favorable opinion or judgment."

Let's consider all those things or people we humans— especially Westerners—regard highly or favorably. If the output of our media provides any clue we see that it is anything *but* a long-term and lasting relationship. We esteem the rich, the beautiful, the famous, and the notorious. We esteem the rebels, those who buck the system, and those who determine their own paths no matter what the consequence. Sadly, our media now esteem not the chaste and virginal (as was societally esteemed as recently as the 1950s) but rather mock virginity and self-control with shows that make virgins (both male and female) laughing stocks. They do so by implication that virgins are too unattractive or socially awkward to attain sexual victory over another. The movie *40-Year-Old Virgin* (though hysterical) comes to mind. In the past, the "loose" woman was indirectly disdained through her portrayal as a Mae West type of "bar broad" who hung out at local taverns while the virtuous and honorable women were elevated and esteemed (Ma Ingalls, June Cleaver, the domestic type).

While I have not bought into the belief that society as a whole now esteems the "experienced" over the "virginal" (a silent majority exists) it is unquestionable our media have. Consider shows like *Jersey Shore* whose only goal is to publicize the sexual escapades of a group of twenty-somethings and elevate its protagonists to a level of celebrity previously garnered by those who usually earned it through talent and hard work. If esteeming someone means to "regard highly or favorably" it is clear that many esteem the celebrities in this show for reasons antithetical to those necessary in happy, long-term marriages.

Another Western value especially detrimental to long-term and thriving marriages is our esteeming of individualism. While this may surprise you, consider the words of scholar Matthew Kelly. In his book *Rediscover Catholicism*, Kelly asserts that one of three major practical philosophies negatively influencing our modern culture today (along with hedonism and minimalism) is individualism. He writes:

When most people today are faced with a decision, the question that seems to dominate their inner dialogue is, "What's in it for me?" This question is the creed of individualism, which is based on the all-consuming concern for self. In the present climate, the most dominant trend governing the decision-making process—and therefore the formation of our cultural belief—system is individualism.

No community, whether as small as a family or as large as a nation, can grow strong with this attitude. Individualism always weakens the community and causes the whole to suffer. In every instance it is a cancerous growth.

The social and political reforms of our age have exalted the individual in a way that is unhealthy for society as a whole. Under the pressure and guidance of a number of special-interest groups that represent only a fraction of society at large, the rights of the individual have been gradually elevated and ultimately placed above the rights of society as a whole. A perfect example is the recent situation in California where a court banned public schools from using "under God" when saying The Pledge of Allegiance because one student found it offensive. The rights of the individual have been strengthened at all costs, with no regard for right and wrong, and often to the detriment of the whole. At the same time, everything has been done to weaken the rights of the Church, the State, and authority of any type.

All this has been done under the banner of false freedom. The false and adolescent notion that freedom is the opportunity to do whatever you want, wherever you want, whenever you want, without the interference of any other person or party. This is not freedom.

Our culture places a very high premium on self-expression, but is relatively disinterested in producing "selves" that are worth expressing.

The fruits of individualism are no secret to any of us:

greed, selfishness, and exploitation. What would become of a family or a nation in which each member adopted individualism as his or her own personal philosophy? (32-33)

So I'd like to take this opportunity to pose one more question than did Kelly. What would become of our marriages if each *spouse* adopted individualism as his or her own philosophy? Oh wait, let me rephrase that. What *has become* of our marriages since we *have focused* more on the individual than the couple? Now, I am American through and through and I love this great nation. I love that I am empowered as a woman to take control of my own destiny, that I am a citizen of the nation to which more people choose to immigrate than any other because they believe it's the modern day "Promised Land." But I am also quick to recognize that this ideological esteeming of "self before other" is poisonous to our culture, our families, and to our marriages.

Crazy isn't it? One of the very principles foundational to our nation's existence is working against the very goals we set for ourselves—one of which is the Super marriage.

But let's continue with this concept of esteeming in our relationships. When I first began to date that suitor of mine, I believed he could do no wrong. Yes, of course I have high intelligence and *know* he is not perfect, but that just confirms my point. While I knew this, I still focused on that which he excelled in—that potential within him that shone so brightly to me that it overshadowed anything he did poorly or in which he might not have excelled. Further, had anyone tried to point out some of his weaknesses, I would have either doubted the degree of those flaws greatly or I would have consciously chosen to disregard them knowing intuitively I'd chosen to define him by his strengths. Going back to our initial definition of esteem it becomes clear that I—like nearly every new couple—regarded highly or favorably my future husband. I regarded him with respect *and* admiration. I esteemed him.

Esteem, like the other qualities of adoration, is something we *choose* to extend to another. As such, we also choose to withhold esteem as well. As with our conversation on honor I am compelled to ask, "When did we *stop* esteeming our spouses?

And why?" It likely eroded little by little with each instance of intentional or unintentional hurt inflicted upon us. Let's face it. We are not perfect. We are *all* going to mess up sometimes. Super Husbands mess up and so do Super Wives. It's an unavoidable fact of life...and love. So what makes the difference? Why do Super spouses continue to esteem one another while so many of us neglect to do so or, worse yet, *choose* to stop esteeming?

The answer might be found by looking backwards. In the initial stages of our relationships, the ability to focus on one's strengths over one's weaknesses is natural and effortless. It could be argued as necessary for mate selection and procreation to be blind to someone's flaws that are immediately visible to others. Only over time as this natural, yet irrational, emotional "high" ebbs, do we begin to see more clearly those things that our mates do poorly. In terms of the promulgation of our species, the ability to see primarily one's good qualities allows us to be "crazy" enough to commit ourselves to one person until the day we die—forsaking all others. But before we apply this concept to our romantic relationships, let's develop it by considering how it applies to our non-romantic relationships.

Members of the Baby Boomer generation (born 1946-1964) and those generations that preceded it were taught to respect authority. Those generations had heroes—leaders they could emulate or look up to. However, members of Generation X (born 1965-1984) found themselves with few heroes as a result of the rebellious spirit of the Sixties that ushered in the era of bucking power and rebelling against authority. Their leaders had failed them and the result was positions of authority alone were no longer reasons for esteeming an institution or an individual. The Millennial Generation (1985-2004) is veritably the first generation that does not look to authority in the traditional sense for its heroes and idols, as did previous generations. This generation believes *they* have just as much authority, power, and (for some) wisdom, as do those older and more experienced. With this generation has come an ideology that rank is no longer esteemed across the board but rather esteem is conferred upon those who have fame and celebrity—for whatever reason—such as any Kardashian, Paris Hilton, and all those who are famous for well, for being famous.

In my younger years (before I'd earned any degrees or associated with people society considers celebrities) I often esteemed people professionally higher than myself who were more educated, more affluent, and who held higher rank than me. Now that I interact regularly with professionals I once esteemed as better than myself, I know they are just like me, have many of the same fears, the same weaknesses, hopes, hurts, as me. The playing field has been leveled in my mind. This happens naturally in our intimate relationships as well. The trick is to understand this is inevitable and use it as a psychological balancing component. It's good to see "celebrities" as no better than me so I can stop being intimidated by them and their status. However, in terms of my spouse it is also good to *re-place* him on a metaphorical pedestal (not compared to me but to other men) and see him (or her) for his good qualities and not his bad. In essence, the same greatness you likely saw when you first started dating.

In the initial throes of our relationships—or the early years of marriage—few of us find it difficult to regard our lovers as anything but highly or favorably. In this early stage it's not that we are lying to ourselves about our lovers but are, rather, *focusing* on that in which they excel and their potential for greatness.

Fast-forward a decade or so and while many other couples have long since stopped esteeming their spouses, Super Couples have not. For reasons that will be explained throughout this book, Super Couples continue "to regard highly or favorably" one another each and every day of their married life. They continue "to regard with respect or admiration" the one with whom they've chosen to spend the rest of their lives. So as you'll learn throughout these pages, esteeming is a choice—the only choice if we want extremely happy marriages. You'll learn that when we esteem the wrong things (fame, fortune, beauty, status) or the wrong people, our relationships struggle. And though we do often esteem wrongly, we still seek the fairytale. We want it all! Relationally speaking, the good news is that we *can* have it all (extreme marital happiness). It's just that for the most part we're going about it the wrong way. We're about to remedy that.

RESPECT

Quite possibly, the lack of respect—the inability or choice not to respect—is the overarching cause of so many of our societal ills today. People no longer *know how* to respect, are not taught *to* respect, nor do they realize the incredible value *of respect* and its power to transform lives. We are witnessing an insidious spreading of disrespect within our nation, communities, families, and marriages, as well as a sad disrespect for ourselves. In terms of our marriages, respect is possibly the number one quality leading to Super. Grow in respect and the rest will return.

When I was younger I had the mantra "respect your elders" beat into my head by my mother. She also taught us to respect authority, respect others, respect others' property, privacy, needs, to respect ourselves and, most of all, she always taught us to respect our differences. As a Girl Scout we were taught by reciting the Girl Scout law "to respect ourselves, others, and authority." Likely, you were taught many of these same things, though as I look back I never truly knew what it meant *to respect*— its definition. Though I couldn't define it, I was certain that if I didn't do it there would be serious motherly ramifications to deal with at home. Four decades later, it has become apparent that somewhere along the way respect has been lost. Consider the growing disrespect for our police in many of our nation's cities. Our political leaders no longer respect each other as witnessed by the vitriol spewed at colleagues from opposing parties. People no longer respect themselves or their bodies as witnessed by the high levels of self-denigration through drug and alcohol abuse, self-mutilation, and sexual promiscuity, just to name a few. Lest I digress too far from the topic, this lack of respect in society has most certainly extended into the realm of marriage.

According to Dictionary.com, respect as a noun is "esteem for or a sense of the worth or excellence of a person, a personal quality or ability, or something considered as a manifestation of a personal quality or ability: *I have great respect for her judgment*; the condition of being esteemed or honored: *to be held in respect*." Further, as a verb several other definitions are listed: "to hold in esteem or honor: *I cannot respect a cheat*; to show regard or consideration for: *to respect someone's rights*;

to refrain from intruding upon or interfering with: *to respect a person's privacy*; to relate or have reference to." So I ask, if I disagree with my spouse's opinions in a particular area can I still respect his/her opinion? Can I still show regard or consideration for his opinions even when I disagree with them as so many of us spouses do with one another?

It is difficult to write a chapter on respect when I can see in my mind's eye the plethora of ways and times I disrespected my husband—both verbally and in my head—and those memories are already convicting me and my contribution to those days of extreme unhappiness in our marriage. I remember consciously thinking that since he verbally shut down on me in private that I'd get him to open up if I brought up the subject in public—just for a response. (He'd ignore my queries and say nothing thinking his silence meant he "wasn't fighting.") Though my ignorance is now blaring it speaks to the desperation I felt in trying to get some response from my husband: to connect, to talk, to answer my questions. I was thinking, *Please help!!! Can you hear me? Somebody please help me get through to this person because I'm dying on the inside!*

Hmm...esteem for or sense of the worth or excellence of my husband, his qualities and abilities...Ouch. Back in 1983 that was easy. Dan loved to cook and was excellent at it (praise God, because my kids call me "Betty-Burn-It-In-the-Microwave." They'd have never made it to adulthood had they relied solely on *my* cooking skills). Dan was the night baker on the ship on which he served and would nightly sneak me home the choicest of his creations "just because." He was extremely handsome, he'd go running with me (though I was faster), he loved his family deeply and made sure I was a part of it. Had you asked me anything about this man any day of 1983 or 1984 I likely would have responded with great esteem for this man and his abilities.

I respected his opinions back then (except in music. He had terrible taste in music). When we chose furniture for our first house and he said he liked a certain style, then I liked that style too. I had my own opinions too, but had no difficulty agreeing with most of his choices because I respected from whom they came. My husband even came into our marriage knowing what names he'd want to give his first girl and boy—so we named our daughter Jessica (and never had the Joshua).

I point out the specifics of my relationship in order for you to recognize the presence or absence of respect in your own relationships. And this holds true for all of your relationships: your parents, colleagues, siblings, friends as well as your spouse. What must become apparent is that respect is so much more than that which we confer upon others in titles such as Mister or Misses, Madame or Sir, Auntie or Uncle, and even Your Highness.

There is a difference between respecting the things one does and says and respecting an individual simply for being a member of the human species. I confer respect upon individuals because of their opinions, their character, their expertise, their knowledge, their morals, their values. I choose not to respect a racist or a philanderer or a criminal. I can respect the essence of their humanness—the immeasurable value of every human because they were made in the image and likeness of God—but I do not, nor cannot, respect the poor way they choose to live their lives or the poor decisions they make.

Respect is the deeper sense of worth or excellence of a person—regardless of most anything else. Fundamentally we are talking about basic human respect—the belief that all people are worthy no matter their status, appearance, ethnicity, or whether or not he is a former inmate or former Miss America. Whether or not one agrees with all the beliefs, attitudes, and values of another, based on this ideological assumption, all persons are worthy of basic human respect. Yet we so often only confer it once it's been earned or when we feel like it.

I remember when in elementary school my report card frequently reported "need for improvement" in the box marked "respects others." Why? Was I a naughty child? No, not at all. The contrary was true: I was a good kid with good grades. But I did not realize I was not respecting others' needs for quiet when I talked out of turn or blurted my answers to questions when others raised their hands first.

For the sake of this lesson, we will not discuss professional respect but only the type needed to maintain healthy and extremely happy intimate relationships. This argument is focused specifically on the sense of worth or excellence of those persons most intimate with us *by choice*—our spouses. Respect as it relates to our marriages, is a choice. Respect is given freely as a gift to the other. When the lack of respect generally becomes problematic is not when we are in agreement with our mate's thoughts, actions, or opinions. That's easy. Our lack of respect is most often born out of our differences: of opinions, of taste, and differences in personalities. I must admit, for someone with a Ph.D. in marriage communication and a life devoted to analyzing it, recognizing disrespect has become second nature. It's effortless at this point. Having once been ignorant of these intangible concepts though, it is easy to see how others remain blind to the presence or absence of respect in their own relationships or those of others.

I'll never forget a reality TV show I watched about a couple planning their wedding. The young man was very passive and his future wife extremely aggressive. They were planning a particular detail about their wedding and when he gave his opinion she embarrassed him right there publicly (and in front of millions of viewers too) by diminishing his opinion. When she responded obnoxiously with a comment such as "Are you kidding me? That's a ridiculous idea!" he simply backed down. He became extremely passive and let her treat him in that manner without standing up for himself. Though the interchange lasted only a minute, the entire interaction was dripping with disrespect. It was so obvious to me I wanted to jump off my couch and contact the show's producer to ask for the name of the couple so I could offer the marital help they were desperately going to need to ensure their marriage survived—and they weren't even married yet!

In the above example it seemed obvious the woman "loved" her fiancé and she may have had basic human respect for him. However, her responses to his opinions showed a lack of respect for those innocuous ways in which they differed: his preference for tuxedos or reception venues for instance. There was nothing inherently *wrong* with his suggestions. They were simply *different*. While I realize I have already addressed that "being different from my spouse" is a faulty assumption of cause for marital breakdown, for the sake of better understanding respect and disrespect in our relationships we will deal with this concept of differences more fully.

As stated earlier, disrespect is not typically a problem until we find areas of *dis*agreement such as in our hobbies, TV shows, music genres, or fashion preferences, etc. For instance, my husband loves deer hunting. I, for one, would rather stick a fork in my eye than to sit in a stinkin' tree for eight hours straight in the freezing or rainy weather in hopes of seeing something to shoot at once every couple of hours (and praying to God I don't miss it). And to do this without being able to go to the bathroom, or, worse yet, unable to *speak* the entire time. Kill me now! Should I *ever* decide to attempt one day in the forest undertaking this mind-numbingly boring activity (which I won't) I would have to have a really good book with me or, my cell phone in order to catch up on my text messaging and emails, or a girlfriend or two with whom to discuss the purpose of all this camouflaged silliness. I am confident I've made my opinions on hunting sufficiently clear at this point. Ugh.

But for my husband, hunting represents everything that is right about this world. While he sits quietly and motionless nestled in his tree of choice high above the earth, escaping all the sights and sounds of twenty-first century life in a bustling city, he feels closer to God, one with nature, and (likely, most importantly) doesn't have to hear his wife's ever-present and nonstop chatter beating like a Morse code on his worn-down eardrums. While hunting, Dan is happiest. (I know, you never saw two more compatible people, right? Sarcasm utterly obvious I hope). In all seriousness, we are simply two very different people who happen to like different things. For decades, during our troubled years, I had presumed these differences were the source of our difficulties. I had nearly convinced myself that two people as different as we were had simply chosen wrong—we were incompatible—and were incapable of ever having a Super marriage because, as I saw it, we could never possibly enjoy doing anything together—I picked the wrong guy. Writing this now, it amazes me how easily we can convince ourselves of whatever we want based on ignorance and a faulty understanding of the truth of a situation. But here's the problem. Whenever my husband chose to hunt, or do anything for that matter that I felt took him away from me or other humans, I attributed it to a character flaw rather than the truth of what it was—a difference in preferences.

As such, I would allow my mind to think horrible things about this man such as "He totally lacks in any personality. He has zero ability to communicate with humans so he has to hide from them in stupid trees all day. If he were a better man like Sally's husband, or Jennifer's boyfriend, he'd be more congenial and spend more time going to parties or cookouts or concerts or... He's such a loser. I can't believe I made such a stupid mistake and married this idiot. Well, maybe I'll outlive him and marry right the next time!"

Wow. Those words embarrass me now. I suppose it's one of the reasons writing this book has been so difficult and why I delayed in doing so for many years. I knew I'd have to face the painful truth of *my* inadequacies in recalling the hurtful thoughts that daily swirled in my head, moving them outside the silent safety of my inner world into the outer world for all to see and judge. But what good would it be for me to be anything less than sincerely forthright with you? The sad truth is I know many of you are reading this because you, too, are in a similar frame of mind with your spouse that I was in those horrible days so many years ago. And for that I am sorry. When anyone's marriage hurts, I hurt. I hurt because as you can see I know the pain of living with someone who caused me so much profound emotional pain and with whom I felt trapped by a piece of paper and the commitment that is marriage. Though that pain no longer exists for me, I remember it well. I could never demean anyone for feeling those same feelings or thinking those same horrible thoughts about their own spouse that I thought about mine as the only means of escaping my pain and one day finding happiness.

Did you recognize the epic levels of disrespect in the above explanation of our different preferences of hobbies? If not, you might be struggling with the same issue in your own relationship. Not specifically the preference for hunting versus hanging out with friends, but seeing your spouse's likes and dislikes—his or her differences from you—in a negative light and judging that to be the problem in your relationship. But how does that happen? How does the same person who once made you happier than any other person in the entire world (so much so you forsook all others and devoted your life to this one alone) become the person whom you now believe makes you most miserable? Did your spouse change that much? Arguably not. What most often changes is not our spouse but our *perception of* our spouse.

The power of perception is life changing. It is foundational to how each of us walks through this life and deals with day-to-day experiences. Perception creates our reality and that includes the reality of a happy or a miserable marriage. In my chapter on the Super Couple Formula, the role of perception on Superness will be discussed in rich detail. For now, know the relationship between perception and respect are strongly interwoven. Super Couples deeply respect one another because of their perceptible esteem for one another and this was seen time and again in interviews. When Pete sought my opinion regarding privacy between couples, he presented an example without assigning positions to either himself or his wife. He did this out of respect for Jenny and a desire to protect her image should my response have sided more with him than her. Like all Super Couples, Pete showed respect through careful word choice. But another way Super Couples show respect is by acknowledging the contributions made by the other.

Lisa mentioned that Jack worked outside the home while she stayed home with their children. Sensing Lisa's feeling she contributed less to the household than did he, Jack perceptibly countered by humorously asserting "Lisa does a great job managing the house, the budget and the kids' activities. I don't know how she does it. I'd be lucky if I could just keep them alive to adulthood." Like Jack, Super spouses praised the other and would show respect by deflecting attention from themselves to their spouse—and this wasn't contrived but very genuine.

I witnessed Super Couples showing respect by honoring their spouse's boundaries. This would be seen quite frequently by the couples I did *not* get to interview. When I'd approach one spouse with my request for an interview I'd frequently see one spouse very interested in doing so but, rather than accept the invitation, the excited spouse would often call me later to politely decline without blaming the other or saying "I'd have liked to but my spouse would not." I consistently saw Super Couples protecting one another's honor in a manner similar to this. Conversely, some spouses would show respect by agreeing to do the interview because it's what their spouses would want.

Duane was a very private man but Gina was a communication expert by trade and because he knew she would love to do the interview and discuss their beautiful "love" he agreed to do so— out of respect.

Respect runs deep in Super marriages and my interviews were rife with examples of the deep respect each husband had for his wife and vice versa. In this society where respect is in dangerous shortage we'd be good to learn from Super Couples. Unlike others, they never forget the sense of esteem or worth of their spouse. They perceive one another as the invaluable individuals that they are and refuse to focus on flaws.

Months after her interview one of my Super Wives asked me "So, what did you find out by interviewing us? Is there a formula?" After responding affirmatively, there was a formula to Superness, I articulated to her what I'd seen and she immediately agreed. Though she lived it, she would not have been able to articulate those same principles made so obvious to me through interviews. Respect, however, was one of the few traits that she and all Super spouses could clearly see. Without respect it is impossible to develop the next essential ingredient expressed by Super Couples—friendship.

FRIENDSHIP

"...We knew that we were best friends before we got married and we didn't want to lose that. We wanted to continue that friendship and that fun." (Chuck, Super Husband)

For all my Super Couples one thing was obvious: they were all friends first. Super came second. Unlike some of the previously discussed elements of Super Couple relationships, this one will be easy to explain. Though in my chapter on faulty assumptions I stated there was no one right way to come together, I must also assert that it is exponentially easier to attain an extremely happy marriage if couples first establish a friendship. While this may sound laughably obvious, friendship is not at the foundation of many marriages because many engage or even marry while their brains are still in the temporary and irrational phase produced by the rush of the "love cocktail." But even for those who made it past this point before they said "I do" many take for granted the value of seeing their mates as friends above and beyond their role as lover or spouse. Although the tide is turning, many still put their spouses in one category and their "friends" in another. This need not be the case—nor should it be.

In every Super Couple interview one spouse would iterate "my spouse is my best friend" or "I would rather hang out with my spouse than any other friend." After recently retiring from the military, Rob and Maggie took a child-free two-week vacation to Europe. Upon returning Maggie said "After twenty years of relative separation I wasn't sure if we'd be able to spend that much time together without driving each other crazy. But now I know we can. We actually *liked* hanging out, seeing things and doing nothing at all, or even just driving in the car. It was so much fun! I'm pretty sure retirement won't be so bad after all." Rob agreed. "We had a blast!"

Of course Rob and Maggie love each other. But at the root of their relationship is a deep friendship—an affection for doing the things with each other that friends do: hanging out, talking about day-to-day events, playing, running errands, grocery shopping, just being together. And they are not alone. Every single couple spoke of their enjoyment of just hanging out with their spouse and desiring that time together over any time with other friends. Lisa and Chad have lunch together nearly every weekday. Chad drives to Lisa's work and waits for her to walk out the door. He said "I still get excited seeing Lisa walk out the door. Sure I have other friends, but Lisa is my best friend. When I have the occasion to go golfing with the guys I still have a good time but the whole time I'm looking forward to going home to Lisa. We just have a lot of fun together." As a matter of fact, both Lisa and Chad told me they usually only make plans with others on days they know they can't spend with each other.

I could go through every transcript and find at least one example that points to their friendship as one of the factors responsible for their extremely happy marriages, but the redundancy would be superfluous. Research has consistently shown that friendship is at the foundation of thriving marriages. The Gottman Institute affirms this when they say "to make a relationship last, couples must become better friends and one of the best ways to become better friends is by 'building love maps,' which is a means of getting to know our spouse's inner psychological world, his or her history, worries, stresses, joys, and hopes." Super Couples are expert at building these love maps that deepen their connections with their spouses. They genuinely like each other and like getting to know each other better daily. Super Couples truly are best friends.

While friendship as a factor in Super marriages might seem obvious, its converse must be considered: why are so many married couples unhappy and *not* friends? Didn't they start out as friends? When and why did those friendships end or weaken? Easily put, many couples stop doing what it takes to maintain friendship. Busyness, children, careers, and the day-to-day drudgery associated with building a home begin to take up so much of the couple's time and energy that in many cases their friendship is taken for granted—and it weakens.

Much like any friendship that weakens when life comes between two people—graduation, relocation, change of employment—when we are no longer able to devote the same amount of time or attention to one another we can no longer build upon our relationships. This is not to say individuals would not enjoy spending time with old friends should they visit as many of our friendships pick up where they left off. With old friends, much of what was held in common initially is still in common today. Additionally, social media have made maintaining friendships much easier than in preceding eras because its users are able to keep abreast of each other's lives. However, the friendship between spouses needs more than the occasional wall post or event photo. The friendship between a married couple is maintained and deepened by sharing daily those things usually only experienced through interaction and conversation: our stressors, joys, issues with our bosses, and even the most trivial of subjects like our favorite TV shows, our hobbies, or our current craving for peppermint ice cream.

With this in mind, it is imperative that date night remains a regular and consistent event on the calendars of all married couples. Going on dates, if only for a two-hour escape from the kids to your favorite ice cream parlor, is an extremely effective means of maintaining solid friendships. As stated above, dates need not include "world-changing" discussion but simply conversation that is fun, playful, or a rehashing of a story from your earlier years of dating and marriage. When questioned, Super Couples agreed that at the root of their friendships were conversation about daily life. Many even labeled themselves as boring married couples and figured I'd not find anything interesting enough to want to interview them. They couldn't have been further from the truth. Interviewing these couples provided a knowledge that the richness of marriage doesn't come from the extraordinary, once in a lifetime moments but from ordinary, everyday occurrences that when shared make an ordinary friendship extraordinary.

COMMUNICATION

Lastly, it should not surprise you to learn that, like friendship, Super Couples all believe communication is key to an extremely happy marriage. Although each rightfully asserted so, when listening to them, their examples pointed more specifically to conversation as the preferred method. Super Couples make time to talk together. Research has shown that before marriage the average couple spends approximately three hours a day talking with one another. It might shock you to learn that after marriage that average drops to a mere fifteen minutes of actual talk time together. Wow. It's no wonder our marriages are failing; we are failing our marriages.

At the very core of marriage is connection, and if we cease to make it a priority, over time that connection weakens and breaks. Tricia and Jim recalled a particular couple of weeks when the chaos of their home was so overwhelming they'd begun to get irritable. Though they weren't snapping at each other, they found themselves on edge. Jim had just started as a partner in his company and Tricia, though also full-time employed (and still extremely supportive of Jim and his career), was taking on most of the household responsibilities including their four elementary and toddler-aged children. Eventually they realized that with Jim coming home at 9:30 many nights they simply hadn't had any time to talk—to debrief and "hash out" some of the things that had been going on all week at work. Once they did, they felt 100% better. Additionally, they agreed early on it was okay to go to bed angry, too. The conversation went as follows:

Tricia: *I think if you had to nail down one of the most important questions in our marriage, it would 100% be communication. I remember early-on dating, we were not engaged yet I think, but you know the old saying of, "never go to bed mad," I always thought that was supposed to be true. You can never go to bed mad because that will just ruin your relationships and he taught me that it's so much better to go to bed mad and talk about it in the morning with a clear head. It was more hurtful to us and our relationship to fight at 11:30 and midnight about something so petty.*

Jim: *Yeah, one or two in the morning, and then you have to wake up and go to work.*

Tricia: *...and you're saying things you don't mean because you're tired.*

Me: *What are some things you've ever said that you didn't mean and how do you keep the damage from happening?*

Tricia: *You walk away for a minute and take a big, deep breath. If we were having some sort of a disagreement in the middle of the day my plan was always "let's talk about it right now and fix it right now." That's how I thought you were supposed to handle stuff. He was more of the "I'm not talking about it with you right now because you're fired up, I'm fired up, we're going to say things we don't mean, and we're going to say things that don't apply. We can talk about it when we're settled down and can have a more rational conversation." It only took a handful of arguments for me to realize that his way was the right way and it worked better for us. I still remember you said that night, "I can't do this" because it was something dumb I'm sure, I don't even know...*

Jim: *I think it was about cleaning.*

Tricia: *Whatever it may have been, it was something that I wanted to talk about right now and I had to have answers right now. He said, "We can go to bed mad, it's okay, we'll talk about it tomorrow when I'm not exhausted, when I've got a clear head, I can think, and answer your questions." And I said,*

"That's fine. If we ever have a fight again I promise you I'll go to bed as long as you promise me first thing after I get off the show, whatever we're doing, we'll drop it, meet each other at lunch and talk about it." He said, "That's fine, let's do that." We never had to do that because we immediately started to communicate properly, without emotions and without getting angry. So communication has been good for us, but as of late we hadn't had the time to communicate.

Jim: *We weren't even fighting.*

Tricia: *Nope.*

Jim: *It was just that we hadn't been communicating.*

Tricia: *I had things I wanted to tell him but I couldn't tell him because by the time he got home he was tired or I had to go do this, or he had to go do that and I'd just be like, "Oh, I'll just tell him later." Until finally a few nights ago I said, "I know it's 9:30 and we're both tired, but can we just talk? We need to, I have a lot of things that I need to talk to you about." He in turn, had a lot of things that he wanted to hash out. So it was a long time in coming.*

Tricia and Jim's example mirrored most every Super Couple. Each knew the value of talking with their spouse even if that conversation was only about day-to-day goings on, as in the example above. In two weeks, they were already recognizing the negative effects of too little marital communication. Fortunately, they heeded the warning signs and made time to reconnect, which immediately produced a positive turnaround in their relationship. A footnote regarding this couple's decision to sometimes "go to bed angry" is in order. Many couples question this rationale, as it seems to contradict the biblical mandate that dictates that persons should "never let the sun go down on their anger." Tricia and Jim, in their example, are not choosing to remain angry at and harbor a grudge with one another by allowing it to fester overnight. The mandate was written to cause others to seek reconciliation, which is exactly what this couple was choosing to do. By waiting until well rested they were deliberately choosing not to avoid an issue, but to deal with it in the most loving and respectful way possible.

Like Tricia and Jim, we need to spend actual time talking and connecting with our spouses. In recent decades the idea has been pushed that "quality time" is better than "quantity time" in terms of connecting with our children and loved ones. While well intentioned, its proponents were also misguided. No child would ever say to his or her parents, "I'm glad that I get to see you only fifteen minutes each day. They're definitely fifteen quality minutes." That child wants more of her parents' time because she knows intuitively that when Mommy or Daddy is with me there is nothing more important to them. I am their priority. He likewise also knows that in those remaining 23 hours and 45 minutes something or someone else is of greater priority.

Time with our spouses is exactly the same. We need quantity to remain as happily together as we were when we were first dating and spent three hours a day together in conversation. That being said, while being together in the same home or room does not mean quality connection is necessarily taking place, conversely, if not in the same home or room together, it is impossible for any meaningful connection to be taking place at all. We need both quantity *and* quality. Of course, I am not referring to those who cannot be together for some reason because they are out of town, on a military deployment, or detained in any way such as in prison and there is no way to be in the same room together. In those cases, the use of social media such as Skype, Facetime, or even phone calls can serve as a very effective substitute means of communicating in person. But remember, taking time to connect over these media (rather than no communication at all) is still a way to show your loved ones they are still a priority and in doing so continues to draw the two of you closer. We humans understand you are giving "me" a precious gift of your hours that you are not giving to anyone else *and* hours you will never get back...and it feels good.

But while Super Couples have shown that talking together *frequently* is good, they have also shown that quantity alone is insufficient. Super Couples make it an imperative to control "how" they say what they say to their spouses. Hundreds of hours of interviews revealed a kindness and gentleness with which Super Spouses conversed with one another—one not usually apparent in average or troubled marriages. If you ever observe couples or families talking you'd notice that many people speak more kindly to colleagues and strangers than to their siblings, parents, or spouses. Familiarity breeds contempt. Sad, isn't it? We give our best selves to those we love least. Not Super Couples, though. Tricia and Jim's example showed the kindness and thoughtfulness involved in "how" Super Couples relate to one another. Tricia was so important to Jim that he lovingly refused to converse or engage in a topic when he knew that conversation would be unproductive and potentially hurtful. For Tricia and Jim (and many happily married couples) going to bed "angry" was not a way to avoid and disrespect one another's need to talk as many unproductive couples do, but rather the opposite, which was shown through his promise to discuss the topic, just at a later time.

During my seminars I will often go over what I call the "Conflict Escalation Model." This model teaches couples to deal with conflict on the "Issue" level rather than escalating it to the "Personality" level where we attack, name call, use sarcasm, rather than dealing with the issue at hand. If we deal with conflict on the personality level too often it will eventually escalate to the "Relationship" level where individuals will no longer connect or communicate with the other because of the history of personality-level attacks. After a series of examples and practice modules I present this question: "Would you ever speak to your grandmother the way you speak to your spouse?" Most are taken aback and wince at the thought. "Absolutely not!" When asked why, they respond with some answer reflecting their deep respect for their grandmothers. Hmm. You love and respect grandma too much to speak to her in an unkind manner but your spouse is fair game?

I'm sorry if some of this just sounds so obvious and inane. After all, isn't speaking kindly to one another something even kindergarteners know? While I do believe we all "know" this, I also know we do not all practice this. After nearly two decades of teaching seminars and college courses I have found that teaching the principles behind the "Conflict Escalation Model" is one of the best received (and needed) of all my lessons. "Aha" moments are witnessed daily as individuals are humbled by their newfound awareness of their ineffective means of communicating with others—especially those they love most.

I remember once when I was visiting my sister (half of a Super Couple) and she had something she really wanted to share with her husband. I don't remember what it was but I remember the concerned look on her face as she was considering how to say it. I remember asking her what the big deal was "Just go tell him what you've got to tell him" and she said, "I want to make sure I say it in just the right way so as not to hurt his feelings." I remember being surprised by her response and thinking "Wow, now there's a novel idea. Choose your words as carefully as possible with the ones you love so you won't hurt them in the least way." I was embarrassed at my own inconsideration as I'd have likely just gone to my husband and blurted out whatever it was I had to say without a single thought as to how that delivery might come across.

So to be extremely happily married, frequent *and* thoughtful communication is essential. However, I'd like to introduce now what is quite possibly one of the biggest reasons for marital communication difficulties: gender. Men and women communicate differently.

Wait. What? They do?

Shocking, I know.

Because of the cross-cultural nature of marriage this problem will, for the most part, persist until we gain a better understanding of those differences and then apply that understanding to substantive changes in how we interact with our spouses on a daily basis.

Gendered communication has been studied for decades by scholars seeking to better understand why we do what we do. Scholars have found that the differences in "how we say what we say" are a product of our differing gendered communication styles. Without detailing every gendered communication difference I will summarize in non-academic terms some of the primary differences.

First, scholars have found that males and females view the purpose of conversations differently. Females use conversation as a means of enhancing social connections, creating relationships, and fostering intimate bonds while males use it to exert dominance, attain status and achieve tangible outcomes. Females tend to be more expressive, tentative, and polite in conversation—especially during conflict communication while males tend to be more assertive, and focused on obtaining power and status.

Additionally, males are more likely than females to offer solutions to problems in order to avoid further seemingly "unnecessary" discussions of interpersonal problems while females, on the other hand, value cooperation, which involves a concern for others, selflessness, and a desire to be at one with others. Females tend to value conversation for the relationships it creates. For females, the process of communication itself is valued. Lastly, females tend to be more social-emotional in their interactions with others, whereas males tend to be more independent, unemotional or detached in conversations.

As you can see, the process of communication is extremely multifaceted. By adding the gender dynamic it becomes even more difficult to put in a neatly defined category. But if we are to have a Super marriage, understanding how and why our spouses operate as they do is imperative. Further, gaining this information will help us better understand ourselves as well, which is quite liberating to those of us struggling just to get to "happy." Men and women don't communicate differently because we feel like it. In truth, our brains predispose us to certain communication styles. We're wired differently. To show this, we're next going to attempt to uncross some of those wires by looking at the gendered brain.

THE GENDERED BRAIN

A large amount of information is already commonly known regarding the differences in the male and female brains. Society and science have long since gotten beyond the previously articulated and erroneous notions of earlier generations that men and women and their brains are pretty much the same and that it is the socialization process alone that forces boys and men to act one way and girls and women to act another. Socialization is definitely a huge contributor to why we act, feel, and think in the ways that we do. We are greatly influenced by socialization and cannot ignore its influences. However, if I treated my daughter and my son in exactly the same ways, said the same words, dressed them the same ways, forced them to play with the same toys and differed in no ways at all in our ways of interacting, the ways that most of the boys would respond would be vastly different from the ways most of the girls would respond to the very same situations. It's a fact. We're different.

When I meet with clients for relationship coaching I spend a large amount of time dealing with gender differences that frequently arise in relationships—and these differences are generally recognized through conflict. When in agreement, there is naturally no need to focus on our ways of interacting. We enjoy the peace with little or no attention paid to our similarities. We just know we're happy. When we disagree, our differences become evident through the friction they cause. Then we notice it. When, in our sessions, I begin to explain how "typical" men's brains are wired and how "typical" women respond in certain situations because of structural and hormonal differences in her brain from a man's brain, there seems to be breathed a mutual sigh of relief from the couple who are instantly educated and validated in their own "ways of behaving" to a point of "so that's why he/she does such and such every time _____ occurs!"

I hope I have been very clear in this book that I am talking about the *majority* of men and the *majority* of women when it comes to most situations and most brains. And yes, there are anomalies—those who are just not the same as *most* others in their category. But I will say it one more time. These brain differences are recognizable between *most* men and *most* women. Don't worry if you are not of the norm. I am sure you will still recognize yourself in many of the differences discussed. The goal is to read this and be better able to not only recognize the differences in your ways of responding from those of your mate's but also to be better able to articulate them to your mate in order to work through areas of conflict.

So now let's talk about some of the very basic brain differences. Of course, new research is coming out daily that can further explain these principles and some are more academic sounding than others. My purpose here is not to explain neural functioning in rich detail because I am not a neuroscientist but rather a social scientist. Further, you likely could not care less about having too many of the finely detailed differences spelled out. However, it is essential to understand some of these basic physiological differences as they apply to husbands and wives and their differing responses to the same stimuli. So I'll do my best to give you the information you need most.

I have decided it best to quote an expert in the field of neuroscience, Louann Brizendine, a neuropsychiatrist and author of the books *The Female Brain* and *The Male Brain* in order to do so. Afterwards, I will overlay the information garnered from my social science and relationship research to offer the most complete picture of how men and women function within (and outside of) Super marriages. In her introduction to *The Male Brain* Brizendine writes:

> Male and female brains are different from the moment of conception. It seems obvious to say that all the cells in a man's brain and body are *male*. Yet this means that there are deep differences, at every level of every cell, between the male and female brain. The male cell has a Y chromosome and the female does not. That small but significant difference begins to play out early in the brain as genes set the stage for later amplification by hormones. By eight weeks after conception, the tiny male testicles begin to produce enough testosterone to marinate the brain and fundamentally alter its structure.
>
> Over the course of a man's life, the brain will be formed and re-formed according to a blueprint drafted both by genes and male sex hormones. And this male brain biology produces his distinctly male behaviors.
>
> ...In the female brain, the hormones estrogen, progesterone, and oxytocin predispose brain circuits toward female-typical behaviors. In the male brain, it's testosterone, vasopressin, and a hormone called MIS (Mullerian inhibiting substance) that have the earliest and most enduring effects. The behavioral influences of male and female hormones on the brain are major. We have learned that men use different brain circuits to process special information and solve emotional problems. Their brain circuits and nervous system are wired to their muscles differently—especially in the face. The female and male brains hear, see, intuit, and gauge what others are feeling in their own special ways. Overall, the brain circuits in male and female brains are very similar, but men and women can arrive at and accomplish the same

goals and tasks using different circuits.

We also know that men have two and a half times the brain space devoted to sexual drive in their hypothalamus. Sexual thoughts flicker in the background of a man's visual cortex all day and night, making him always at the ready for seizing sexual opportunity. Women don't always realize that the penis has a mind of its own for neurological reasons. And mating is as important to men as it is to women. Once a man's love and lust circuits are in sync, he falls just as head over heels in love as a woman—perhaps even more so. When a baby is on the way, the male brain changes in specific and dramatic ways to form the daddy brain.

Men also have larger brain centers for muscular action and aggression. His brain circuits for mate protection and territorial defense are hormonally primed for action starting at puberty. Pecking order and hierarchy matter more deeply to men than most women realize. Men also have larger processors in the core of the most primitive area of the brain, which registers fear and triggers protective aggression—the amygdala. This is why some men will fight to the death defending their loved ones. What's more, when faced with a loved one's emotional distress, his brain area for problem solving and fixing the situation will immediately spark. (2-5)

Okay. Aren't you glad *that lesson* is over? Well now it's time to make sense of it. First of all, isn't it amazing to see all of the different things going on in men's and women's brains? That alone should illuminate the fact that since our brains and hormonal production are different from one another, then of course how we interact in the world and in our marriages on a daily basis is also going to be greatly affected by these differences. Again, if you want an extremely well-articulated, more neurologically detailed explanation of the differences between the male and female brains, I would suggest you read Brizendine's books in their entirety. I found these two books extremely intriguing and well written. They gave me an enormously clear understanding of why we do what we do from a physiological standpoint. There are others of course, but these are two of my favorites.

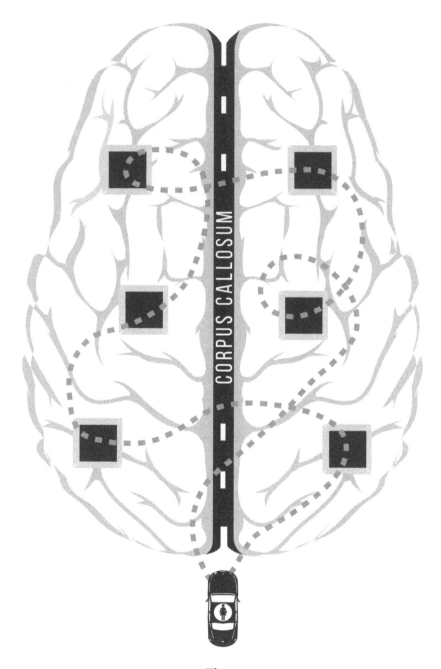

Fig. 1

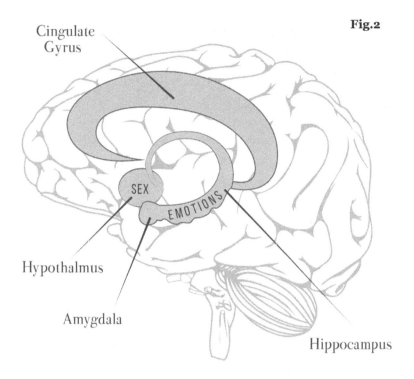

Fig.2

Cingulate Gyrus

SEX

EMOTIONS

Hypothalmus

Amygdala

Hippocampus

   While each of the different brain sections and hormonal influences affect our behaviors in different ways, for the sake of explaining how Super Husbands and Super Wives interact, I am going to focus primarily on two areas: the two hemispheres (gray matter) and the corpus callosum (white matter) as well as two hormones: testosterone and oxytocin. I will be explaining them in as minimal detail as necessary to make clear the factors that lead to Superness. Let's start with the hemispheres—the gray matter—where the brain gets its functioning power. We all have the left hemisphere, and the right hemisphere, each of which houses an amygdala—the emotion center—and is responsible for processing most of the emotional function. Between the two hemispheres is the corpus callosum, which I lovingly refer to as the freeway system that sends messages from the right hemisphere to the left and vice versa. For the most part, the hemispheres speak to each other. The left hemisphere's messages toggle back and forth between both sides of the brain as well as do those messages originated in the right hemisphere. Pieces of information on one side connect to other pertinent messages and memories on the other. Logic and emotions interact. Connections and relationships are made between one situation, thought, or emotion to what might otherwise seem a wholly unrelated thought, situation, or emotion.

However, at about eight weeks gestation the male baby's brain is inundated with testosterone and that testosterone singes the pathways in the corpus callosum, thereby prohibiting (to greater or lesser degree) the left brain and the right brain from speaking to one another. As such, we can envision the male brain as having compartments—each one separate from the other— where the different compartments do not touch or interfere with one another. Therefore, if the male is dealing with a particular topic he goes to the particular "compartment" in the particular hemisphere of his brain that deals with that topic and generally stays there until that "conversation" or "situation" comes to some sort of resolution before he moves on (comfortably) to another situation and another part of his brain (which takes about twenty minutes). A fairly common way of saying this is that the typical male brain is much more compartmentalized than is the female brain. As such, when he is dealing with the kids he goes to the kid compartment or box. When dealing with the job he goes to the job box. When dealing with the finances he goes to the finance box. When dealing with the in-laws he goes to the in-law box. When focusing on sports he goes to the sports box, and so on. Of course, whenever I am teaching one of my seminars the question that inevitably comes up next, albeit tongue and cheek much of the time, is "Does a male then not use his whole brain?" Ha-ha ladies. Of course he does. But unlike the typical woman, the typical man uses only one part of his brain at a time. Some of these "boxes" or compartments to which he must go at any given time are in the right hemisphere and some are in the left hemisphere. He goes to whichever part is needed for a given situation. It's much more of a linear way of processing information or situations. This explains why most men can be so single-minded. And thank God they can be because women, for the most part, are all over the place.

Women's brains are not so linear and sequential in their processing of information as are male brains. Because the female had no such "singeing" of the neural pathways in her corpus callosum as did men, her left and right hemispheres continue to constantly speak to one another. Connections exist from any one subject to myriad other subjects. It's not very linear or sequential at all. Women will often start out discussing family and then progress through their favorite sitcoms, shoe shopping, and world peace all within the same conversation—without ever having had to "solve" anything. Each topic can easily connect to the other and even if the topics might seem unrelated to men, the female brain will have little difficulty making connections between them.

To men who might be observing a female conversation, it might seem as if they begin by opening the top drawer of the dresser then quickly go to the middle drawer, then run across the room all the way to the armoire and open the bottom middle drawer before quickly being forced to race back to the dresser to reopen the initial drawer that began the conversation. It happens so fast that the man runs frantically around the room opening drawers and (attempting) to shut each before another is opened only to eventually give up at the impossible challenge, leaving a room in chaos with half-opened drawers strewn with unfolded clothing and thus he just throws himself face up on the bed with a television remote in his hands to speed him to his nothing box to rest from the overexertion. It's exhausting.

The male brain seeks desperately to "finish" or "close" one compartment before moving onto the next while women do this effortlessly—this is the reason most women are typically better at multitasking than are most men. Keeping this vision in your head, it is for this reason that females, usually unknowingly, often overwhelm the males in their lives when having a "normal" conversation with them. He's trying to decide into which compartment he needs to enter in order to engage this conversation with you (and fix whatever it is that you are talking about) and yet he is often left woefully lost and frustrated when no single compartment is determined or sufficient for the conversation. When this happens, the male brain is "flooded" by a rush of chemicals that attempt to shut down this overstimulation (excessive emotional arousal) as a matter of protection. Women experience no such flooding until a significantly higher state of emotional arousal has been reached. John Gottman, the grandfather of all marriage research, has produced myriad studies regarding this flooding and its effects on the male brain. If you are interested in a more scholarly explanation of what I am about to discuss you should attempt to read as much of it as possible to help fill in some of your own gaps in understanding of male and female differences. I will, however, provide this example of the differences in male and female conversation in order to better exemplify this point. Ladies, pay special attention to the quick topic changes to envision just how quickly we can overwhelm the single-focused male brain.

I just met a girlfriend at a local coffee shop. She had just passed her qualifying exams for her Ph.D. and we met to celebrate. The conversation started out like this:

"Tell me all about it. How was the defense? What did this professor say and that professor do?"

As she started answering the questions she mentioned that she had just gotten off the phone telling her mother all about the defense and then the conversation changed directions to "Where does your mother live? How many other kids does she have? Oh really? She's that much older than you? Why did she have kids so late in life?"

The conversation trajectory then changed to a discussion of family and upbringing.

"Really? Your mother only has an eighth grade education? My mom only has a tenth grade education. Wow! We have so much in common. My mom grew up in Milwaukee...actually, so did I and I am going to do one of my Super Couple seminars there this November."

"You're from Milwaukee? My brother lives there right now. What a coincidence."

"In what part of Milwaukee does he live? I'm doing my seminar at the Marcus Center in Downtown."

"He lives right there in the Marquette area."

"That's right near where I will be. You should tell him he needs to attend my seminar."

"Well, actually I will. He's divorced and currently living with his girlfriend. I won't be able to convince him, but I will be able to convince her. She can get him to do anything."

"Why did he divorce? Was there someone else involved?"

You get the picture. While the conversation started out on one topic—her qualifying exams—it changed directions about six times from our parents, to our home cities, to our siblings, to relationships, to seminars, and so on. As women, there was no difficulty in doing this whatsoever. We were on the same page and able to follow each other's train of thought as they progressed from topic to topic. We were "making connections" or relationships between topics—every topic related in some way to the next topic and then off we went, down another trail. In between these conversational changes we'd often circle back to one of the aforementioned topics and pick up where we left off. Some topics were "finished" but most were not. This was a very circular conversation. By a male or linear perspective, few, if any, of the topics we discussed were "completed" or discussed from beginning to end, and we were fine with that. Finishing them was not necessarily our purpose in coming together. Connecting—or relating—with one another was more important. If there were any compartments in our brains (see Fig. 1), our conversations simply passed through them on their way to and through other compartments and topics much like a train that passes through different cities on route to numerous destinations.

Through this example I hope you are now clearer how women can absolutely drive men nuts when trying to share a conversation with them. While men might be absolutely desirous of following our thoughts in order to process what we are saying (because they love us or care about us and want to please us), they are trying to follow a linear sequence of thoughts. Women are typically anything *but* linear. When we connect one topic to another too quickly we lose them. *"Ok babe. I'm here for you. I'm in the "qualifying exam compartment" for you. I am all yours. I'm in. Fully focused. Let's talk. Hey wait, what? I thought we were talking about the qualifying exams? Are we finished with that now? Oh, okay. Wait? Now we're talking about our parents? Let me go to the "parents" compartment. Okay. Ready. Let's talk about our parents. Wait. Whoa! I thought we were talking about our parents? Why on earth are we now talking about the bills? Or the kids? Did we finish that conversation? Did we finish any of these conversations? Where the heck are we going with this? Get to the point. Tell me the*

freakin' point of this conversation so I can answer it (resolve it) and be done with it!
  Tuned out.
  You see, women aren't attempting to annoy the heck out of men when we converse, though that is what often happens — especially if we are unaware of these neural differences between the male and the female brains and our ways of processing information and communicating. And I haven't even *begun* to address the hormonal influences yet. I know I had no idea of these differences when I was a young and stupid newlywed talking to my husband faster than a jackhammer on concrete. Clearly it had to be *his* problem for not "listening" well enough or not "caring" enough to do so.
  Before I end this chapter I'd like to add one more bit of information to complete this conversation on communication. It might seem that much of this section was devoted to telling women how we communicate in a manner that is unappealing to men and their ways of communicating—as if we are the problem and should curtail our style of communicating to better match the male style. That is not at all what I sought to do. As a scholar/speaker in the field of marriage communication I am completely cognizant of the fact that most of my readers are initially females. I say initially because it is generally the woman who has registered the couple in the seminar or picked up this book first, but she soon either hands it to her man to read or she reads it to him to help him better understand her and what she's been unsuccessfully trying to say herself.
  So I'm addressing much of this chapter to "us women" first so that we can have our own personal "aha" moments and thus gain an awareness of our need to amend our communicative behaviors in order to be better heard and understood by members of the male species. But men are not exempt either. Part Four will extend this learning into actual and practical ways for men (and women) to communicate as Super Couples do. Each of us must adapt our ways to better meet the communicative needs of the other. For now, our greatest imperative has been to illuminate that communication is an extremely important contributor to marital Superness and one that can only be overlooked with dire relational consequences.

During my research, I heard Super Couples say the main ingredients in achieving and maintaining an extremely happy marriage are: kindness, honor, esteem, respect, friendship, and communication. In Part III we will address something that will likely astound the masses: that which was *not* considered a main ingredient in Super Couple marriages.

Part III:

WHAT I DID *NOT* HEAR!

DEFINING LOVE—WHAT IT'S NOT

It may surprise you to find out that when asked *"What, to you, are the main ingredients of Super Couple marriages?"* not one person answered "love." Not one. While this might at first seem ridiculous, after devoting a bit of thought to this idea that love isn't what makes a couple extremely happy it begins to make sense. After all, aren't *all* couples supposedly "in love" when they marry? If "love" is what makes us extremely happy then why would we ever stop loving?

So why would we need a chapter to explain something that is *not* directly responsible for a Super marriage? Easy. Because everyone else thinks love is the answer. This chapter is about to answer that by digging deeply into and breaking down the concept of "love" for once and for all. This is great news because once we know what something is—in this case, love—only then are we able to pursue it, find it, and maintain it in all of our intimate relationships—all of them. And not just a superficial love, but a passionate, faithful, and—dare I say—spiritual love.

Of the three basic tenets of adoration that we discussed in the previous chapters—esteem, respect, and love—love is without a doubt the most problematic to define. This might seem a curious assertion to most readers as certainly love is the most well-known of the three, or so we think. Certainly, love is one of the most used and discussed words and concepts in our societies, homes, workplaces and relationships. And undoubtedly love, along with its counterpart, happiness, is absolutely the most desired and sought after state of being for nearly every human being. However, this definition is the most problematic not because the definition is too difficult to grasp but rather because of one very obvious omission from the 21st Century dictionary definition.

Words appear and disappear because times change and, more importantly, ideologies change. Older words are no longer used because the symbols and ideas they represent are also no longer used. As such, the words are then just removed from the dictionary. Consider a few that are well on their way to extinction now like 8-track, record player, and groovy. In other cases, the words remain in our vernacular but their meanings change. Love is one of those words.

Dictionary definitions of the word *love* abound. In the most recent dictionaries of this third millennium love is defined as "a profoundly tender, passionate affection for another person." Love is "a feeling of warm personal attachment or deep affection, as for a parent, child, or friend." Love is "sexual passion or desire." Love is "a person toward whom love is felt; a beloved person; a sweetheart." Love is "used in a direct address as a term of endearment, affection, as in 'Would you like to see a movie, Love?'" Do you see the problem here? When compared to both esteem and respect, which are defined as both nouns and verbs—a thing *and* an action, love is now in this "new and improved" modern century only defined as a noun.

Now before you Google this I will share that dictionary. com does now list a definition of love that it *calls* a verb (which grammatically speaking it is). However, the verbs of "love" that are listed are used only in conjunction with an object signifying that love is not something that we *do* but something we *have*— pointing it back to the noun. The definitions used are: To *have* love or affection for; to have a profoundly tender, passionate affection for; to have a strong liking for; take great pleasure in; to need or require; benefit greatly from. In these definitions, love is still listed as an object (noun) to be had or possessed, much unlike the definitions of respect or adoration which requires us to *do* something to or for another person.

So again, love is quite possibly one of the most often spoken words in the English language (and probably most every other major language). Certainly, in most every Western nation this would seem to hold true. And so as a researcher I must admit that I was astounded to note that among the plethora of dictionary definitions of the word *love* offered, not one single definition of the word "love" as a *verb* was listed. The implications for this are tremendous in terms of our modern conceptions of love—especially as it relates to marriage. But before I begin to breakdown the definition of what love *is*, let me begin by sharing what love is NOT.

ROMANTIC LOVE

I recently saw a video of a man who surprised his wife of seven months by returning back to the states from military deployment earlier than she had expected. This woman thought she was chosen randomly from the audience to play a game during an inning change at a baseball game but what really happened is the announcer talked about her husband and asked her what message she would send to him right now if he were watching. As she spoke he then appeared from behind her and of course the couple hugged, kissed, and the woman cried in front of a cheering stadium of onlookers who were so happy for this couple. What a romantic gesture and great surprise. What woman wouldn't want this kind of treatment? (Ok, what extraverted woman would not want this kind of a surprise?) Introverted women would still love to be showered with the attention but in a much more private manner with significantly fewer onlookers. But this young twenty-something bride experienced great happiness in that moment. But is her marriage continually happy in every moment? Is there peace and joy in her marriage? Is there *love* in their every interaction? Quite likely since their marriage was less than a year old when this romantic surprise took place there existed a frequent experience of loving feelings between this bride and her husband. Having only been together two-and-a-half years on the day of the surprise their neophyte relationship, yet untested by time, was fresh and new and had not yet withstood any major difficulties. What we saw on the outside may not always be a true reflection of what is taking place inside the relationship. From the outside they seemed extremely happy. They were both smiling, she was crying, they continued to hug and kiss, the audience stood in their ovation towards the couple and the romantic "display" of their love for one another. The fans were truly happy for them because we all, at heart, wish for the fairytale—if not in our own lives then certainly in someone else's. This couple was happy. This couple was "in love." But is there love in their every moment? If one believes in the concept of love being nothing more than a *feeling* then possibly—though their imperfect humanity would still require me to say it is highly unlikely. Most importantly, is their marriage Super? I'll get to that.

So is this love? And, if not, what is love?

Let me begin by discussing the word "love" and the morphing of its definition over time. I began this chapter with the most recent definitions of love found in the dictionary—the noun-only definitions. After getting over my shock at the blaring void in this definition I set out on a historical linguistic excavation of sorts in order to discover if this were always the case. So I went to the library and looked for the oldest dictionaries I could find.

The oldest I found (without having to pay exorbitant amounts of monies digging through archives as far back as the stone tablets chiseled by Moses) was the oldest English dictionary ever written. It was penned in 1755 by Samuel Johnson and entitled *A Dictionary of the English Language*. In it I found something completely converse to its 259-year younger counterparts: it began with love as a verb. This in and of itself is much more significant than one may initially believe because dictionary definitions are generally ordered by the most accepted and most oft used to the least accepted understandings of words. Listing the verb *to love* before the noun *love* points to an early understanding that love is not something we *have* or an object but rather something that we *do*. Just so that you, too, do not have to dig for yourself, I have excerpted below the definitions written in that first dictionary. In addition to the definitions, the sources Johnson found to make his assertions are also listed below, just as they were in 1755:

To LOVE:
1. *To regard* with passionate affection, as that of one sex to the other.
   Good shepherd, tell this youth what 'tis to *love*.
   ~It is to be made all of fights and tears;
   It is to be made all of faith and service;

It is to be all made of fantasy,
All made of passion, and all made of wishes;
All adoration, duty, and obedience;
All humbleness, all patience, all impatience,
All purity, all trial, all observance. *Shakespeare, As You Like It.*
I could not *love* I'm sure One who in love were wise. *Cowley.*
The jealous man wishes himself a kind of deity to the person he loves; he would be the only employment of her thoughts. *Addison's Spectator, N. 170.*
2. *To regard* with the affection of a friend.
None but his brethren he, and sisters, knew, whom the kind youth preferred to me, and much above myself I loved them too. *Cowley.*
3. *To regard* with parental tenderness.
He that loveth me shall be loved of my father, and I will *love* him, and will manifest myself to him. *John xiv. 21.*
4. To be pleased with.
Fish used to salt water delight more in fresh: we see that salmons and smelts *love* to get into rivers, though against the stream. *Bacon's Nat. History. No 703.*
5. *To regard* with reverent unwillingness to offend.
Love the Lord thy God with all thine heart. *Deut. Vi. 5-* (pgs. 1229-1230).

Now I know you likely didn't pick up this book to get an English lesson so I ask for your patience as I feel our lack of understanding of the words we choose is a large part of our problem. Our discourse creates meaning just as your discourse with your spouse while you were dating was so meaningful that you decided to marry. Words are powerful. So if one's words create confusion or are unclear their meanings become convoluted or...meaningless. For instance, if I place a fish in your hand and tell you it's a bird and then in another sentence tell you that birds know how to fly then you'd be confused as you'd be hard-pressed to get that thing in your hand to ever do little more than fall to the ground should you toss it into the air expecting it to fly. It would create quite an argument with any person who's actually seen a real bird because that person would either fight to the death with you (verbally) that birds actually do fly, or he would disregard you as a nut case and move on. The words we give objects have great meaning and thus we choose those words that best meet our communicative needs at any given point.

Next, looking more deeply at Johnson's definitions of the verb to love we notice that nearly all of them begin with the words *to regard* which mean "to look upon or think of with a particular feeling; to have or show respect or concern for; to think highly of; to look at." If we were to substitute any one of the definitions of the word *to regard* into Johnson's definitions of *to love* they would read something like this:

1. *To think highly of* with passionate affection, as that of one sex to the other.
2. *To think highly of* with the affection of a friend.
3. *To think highly of* with parental tenderness.
4. To be pleased with.
5. *To think highly of* with reverent unwillingness to offend.

Or how about this: *To have or show respect or concern for [another person] with reverent unwillingness to offend.* Now I'd say that is a substantially more powerful way to define love in clearly understandable terms. Keep this definition in mind, as we will come back to it. Further, by using the words *to think of* in our reference to love points to the truth that love begins not in the heart but rather in the mind. Thoughts cultivate feelings. Loving thoughts beget loving feelings. Paradoxically, unloving thoughts beget unloving feelings. That is, our loving thoughts about another are what cause us to "fall in love" while our unloving thoughts are the catalyst for our "falling out of love."

Before I go too far down this path of what love is based on these definitions of the verb *to love,* let me first continue with Johnson's definitions of love as a noun. He continues with the following:

1. The passion between the sexes.
2. Kindness; good-will; friendship.
3. Courtship.

4. Tenderness; parental care.
5. Liking; inclination to: as, the *love* of one's country.
6. Object beloved.
7. Lewdness.
8. *Unreasonable liking*. [Italics mine].
9. Fondness; concord.
10. Principle of union.
11. Picturesque representation of love.
12. A word of endearment.
13. Due reverence to God.
14. A kind of silk stuff. (I am very curious what this definition refers to.)

Now Johnson's definitions of love as a noun still necessarily connect love to passion and sex as do our current definitions, but notice also the inclusion of the noun "love" to the noun "kindness," which essentially points to love as still requiring the action of being kind to another person; or love as courtship that also implies the action of courting another that is "paying special attention to (someone) in an attempt to win their support or favor." So even as a noun, Johnson's three-hundred-year-old definition requires the act of focusing one's efforts on pleasing another human being in order to win that person's heart.

Though I will not bore you with an entire chapter of dictionary definitions, my researcher's curiosity beckoned me to probe more deeply to find out just how a definition of one simple word can go from one that foremost calls it an action that takes place between persons to one that completely negates any action taking place and then changes it to nothing more than a feeling one experiences. Did this happen all at once or was it gradual? Of course like any other cultural or societal shift in ideologies this morphing of definitions also took place over a period of three centuries. In order to help you see this transition more clearly I will take you on a quick morphological journey that will help you place in historical context when and how *love* went from an action to a feeling. The transition was no less dramatic than what changes the caterpillar into a butterfly.

The first major transition took place just over a century after Johnson published his dictionary when Webster in 1884 began his definition of love first as a noun rather than a verb. In it love was defined:

> **Noun:** Act of loving, preeminent kindness or devotion to another; affection; courtship; devoted attachment to one of the opposite sex; fondness; devotion; the object of affection; moral good-will; kindness; charity; Cupid, the god of love. (Notice the requirements of action in these noun definitions?)
>
> **Verb.t.:** to be pleased with, be fond of, like; to have good will toward; to have a strong affection for; have a tender feeling toward; to delight in, with exclusive affection.
>
> **Verb i.:** To delight, take pleasure, be in love. To love (referring to covetousness) (pg. 332).

Though in these definitions love is first listed as nouns notice that several of the definitions still point toward the required actions involved in *loving* another person. Now jump ahead nearly forty years to the onset of the Roaring Twenties. While Funk and Wagnall's definition in 1920 returns the verb *to love* to the priority position in their dictionary, it is here that we see love becoming a more sensual verb than it was in the previous dictionaries with its fourth definition that invokes caressing and physical touch:

> **Verb**: To have a feeling of affection or tender regard for. 2. To regard with the affection that is characteristic of the sexual relation. 3. To take pleasure or delight in. 4. To caress; to have a feeling of yearning affection or tenderness or passion inspired by the sexual relation (pg. 473).

No more does it list the verbs that require something to be done *to* or *for* another human being, but now the action merely begins to point toward the more self-focused action of *having* (possessing) a feeling for another—most specifically a sexual feeling. Funk and Wagnall's definitions of love as a noun begin to invoke craving, possession, and animalistic passion:

> **Noun**: A strong complex emotion or feeling causing

one to appreciate, delight in, and crave the presence or possession of the object and to please or promote the welfare of that object; devoted affection or attachment. 2. Specifically, such feeling between husband and wife or lover and sweetheart. 3. One who is beloved; a Sweetheart. 4. Animal passion. 5. A personification of the love = passion: Cupid.

Though Funk and Wagnall list the virtues of love as a noun, there is still an element of other-centeredness retained in its definition that purposes the *feeling* of love as directed at one's desire *"to please or promote the welfare of the object."*

Included in the Funk and Wagnall dictionary is a list of numerous synonyms for love likely included to help clarify its meaning though here it can be argued that love's transition to that of a feeling or noun only began to convolute or cloud our understanding of love. The synonyms it lists are:

Synonyms: Affection, attachment, attraction, charity, devotion, esteem, feeling, fondness, friendship, liking, passion, regard, tenderness. *Affection* is kindly feeling, deep, tender, and constant, going out to some person or object, being less fervent and ardent than love. Love is the yearning or outgoing of soul toward something that is regarded as excellent, beautiful or desirable; love may be briefly defined as strong and absorbing affection for and attraction toward a person or object. Love may denote the sublimest and holiest spiritual affection, as when we are taught that "God is love." Charity has so far swung aside from *this original meaning* that probably it never can be recalled (compare BENEVOLENCE). The Revised Version uses *love* in place of *charity* in 1 *Cor.* 13, and elsewhere. *Love* is more intense, absorbing and tender than *friendship*, more intense, impulsive, and perhaps passionate than *affection;* we speak of fervent *love,* but of deep or tender affection, or of close, firm, strong friendship. Love is used specifically for personal affection between the sexes, in the highest sense, the love that normally leads to marriage, and subsists throughout all happy wedded life. Love can never properly denote mere animal passion [*Author's comment: funny, because this is exactly what has taken place in our modern vernacular and understanding of love!*] which is expressed by such words as appetite, desire, lust. One may properly be said to have love for animals, for inanimate objects, or for abstract qualities that enlist the affections, as we speak of love for a horse or a dog, for mountains, woods, ocean, or of love of nature, and love of virtue. Love of articles of food is better expressed by liking, as love, in its full sense, denotes something spiritual and reciprocal, such as can have no place in connection with objects that minister merely to the senses (pg. 473).

Fast forward a mere thirty-six years after Funk and Wagnall's publication, the Second World War now a decade behind us (including a significant transition of women and men's roles in the home and in the workplace) Daniel Webster in 1956 flip flops once again the definition of love as a noun to the priority position. Curiously, Webster, unlike his predecessors, re-adds mention of God and His association to love that had been absent from definitions for the two hundred years preceding it since Johnson's first English dictionary in 1755. While I am not a historian, one might question whether this re-insertion was due to a post-war mindset that found a surge in Americans who were calling upon God with a renewed fervency that was, prior to the Great Depression and WWII, merely lukewarm. In Webster's dictionary of 1956 he writes:

Noun: 1. A feeling of strong personal attachment induced by sympathetic understanding, or by ties of kinship; ardent affection. 2. The benevolence attributed to God as being like a father's affection for his children; also men's adoration of God. 3. Strong liking; fondness; good will; as, love of learning; love of country. 4. Tender and passionate affection for one of the opposite sex. 5. The object of affection; sweetheart. 6. Cupid or Eros as god of love; sometimes Venus. 7. In Christian Science, a synonym of God.
Verb: 1. To have or manifest love for. 2. To take

delight or pleasure in; as to love books. 3. To show love for by caressing. (verb i.) To have the feeling of love, especially for one of the opposite sex; to be in love (pg. 498).

In this version, though love is still defined as both noun *and* verb, the verb is merely distinguishable as such by its pointing to the possession of a feeling—of course, too, the onset of love as a form of objectification of another. Few actions in order to *show* love are listed. Actually, the only definition that points to love as an *action*—that is, something one must *do* to show love, is in definition 2 "to show love for by caressing." This definition more accurately begins to point to an expression of love in a more physical or sexual manner only, though caressing can also be used as an action to *express* nonsexual feelings of love—as a mother caresses her child or as one caresses another as a means of consoling.

A decade later Webster, in 1964, revises his definitions:

Noun: 1. A strong affection for or attachment or devotion to a person or persons. 2. A strong liking for or interest in something: as, her love of acting. 3. A strong, usually passionate, affection for a person of the opposite sex. 4. The person who is the object of such an affection; sweetheart, lover. 5. Sexual passion or its gratification. 6. Cupid or Eros as the god of love. 8. In theology a) God's benevolent concern for mankind. b) Man's devout attachment to God. c) The feeling of benevolence and brotherhood that people should have for each other.
Verb t.: 1. To feel love for. 2. To show love for by embracing, fondling, kissing, etc. 3. To delight in; take pleasure in: as, she loves good music.
Verb i.: To feel the emotion of love; be in love. Fall in love: to begin to love; feel a strong, usually passionate affection (pg. 868).

Like his predecessors, Webster then goes on to list synonyms for the word *love* as well:

Synonyms: love implies intense fondness and deep devotion and may apply to various relationships or objects (sexual love, brotherly love, love of one's work, etc.); **affection** suggests warm tender feelings, usually not as powerful or deep as those implied by love (he has no affection for children); **attachment** implies connection by ties of affection, attraction or devotion, etc. and may be felt for inanimate things as well as for people (an attachment to an old hat); **infatuation** implies a foolish or unreasoning passion or affection, often a transient one (an elderly man's infatuation for a younger girl) (pg. 869).

Webster's most notable changes include replacing in his definitions of love as a verb from *having* love to *feeling* love. Further, his synonyms now begin to point toward a perversion of love as an elderly man's infatuation for a younger girl. No wonder we as a people are so confused about what it means to love another human being. If we begin to associate merely having a physical feeling, reaction, or arousal for another person as love, then clearly it illuminates how it has become easier to accept and condone other unloving acts as "acceptable" under the guise of "love."

Lastly, in our post-Sixties "If it feels good, do it" culture of free love and sexual expression and post Seventies culture dubbed the "Me Generation," which ushered in the era of no-fault divorce, a decision that stripped couples of the responsibility *to act* in a loving manner toward one's spouse, the *American Heritage Dictionary* in 1982 defines love accordingly:

> **Noun:** 1. an intense affectionate concern for another person. 2. An intense sexual desire for another person. 3. A beloved person. Often used as a term of endearment. 4. A strong fondness or enthusiasm for something: *a love of the woods.* 5. *Capital L* Eros or Cupid, the god of love in classical mythology. 6. *Theology* a) God's benevolence and mercy towards man. b) Man's devotion to or adoration of God. c) the benevolence, kindness or brotherhood that man should rightfully feel toward others. 7. *Capital L. Christian Science.* God.
>
> ***To fall in love.*** *To become enamored or sexually attracted to someone.*

Verb: 1. to feel love for. 2. To desire (another person) sexually. 3. To embrace or caress. 4. To like or desire enthusiastically; delight in. 5. To thrive on; need: *the cactus loves hot, dry air* (pg. 772).

In these definitions and examples the continuation of love acting only as a feeling persists. Further, in the synonyms listed in the *American Heritage* definitions we begin to see where love begins to take on its current conception that one "falls into and out of" love uncontrollably—that we are powerless to escape its influence:

Synonyms: *love, affection, devotion, fondness, infatuation.* These nouns refer to feelings of attraction and attachment experienced by persons. *Love* suggests a feeling more intense and less susceptible to control than that associated with the other words of this group. *Affection* is a more unvarying feeling of warm regard for another person. *Devotion* is dedication and attachment to a person or thing: contrasted with *love*, it implies a more selfless and often a more settled feeling. *Fondness*, in its most common modern sense, is rather strong liking for a person or thing. *Infatuation* is extravagant attraction or attachment to a person or thing, usually short in duration and indicative of folly or faulty judgment (pg. 772).

In this final synonym we see where infatuation most closely defines what many now refer to as love (though few who are "in love" would think at the time that it is faulty or of folly). We connect love to that initial stage of passion when, if not attached to a desire to act in a certain way toward someone, is only short-termed. Keep this in mind as we get into our later chapter on happiness, which explains the differences between self-centric and other-centric happiness. For now we begin to see how the two become entangled, confused, and misused.

Jump ahead yet another thirty-plus years into the new millennium where the oft-used (albeit only partially regarded as tongue-in-cheek) phrase "It's all about me" has become as common a phrase as "How are you?" and we now have a clearer understanding of why dictionary writers ultimately concluded that love is nothing more than a good feeling to be felt and thus erased any requirement of loving actions from their definitions. So where does that leave us? Is romantic love actually "love" or is it simply a state of being that is chosen by two people who feel really good with, about, and in the presence of each other? In order to answer that, let's continue to clarify a bit more about what love is not.

LOVE AS A FEELING

"I love you because you make me feel good." But what happens when that feeling goes away? Likely the persons who have spoken the phrase "I love you but I'm not in love with you" are indirectly referring to this problematic linguistic change in the definition of love because the phrase is illuminating the obvious difference between love as a feeling and love as an action—the noun and the verb. Now, I love the feeling of being in love, who doesn't? All other difficulties seem to disappear into this cloud of joy and happiness that envelopes us when we are "in love" with another human being.

Let me provide an example. A male family member of mine and his first wife were beginning the process of their divorce. During a conversation with his now ex-wife she said to me "There's nothing I can do. I was powerless to save it. I just fell out of love." Of course being the hopeful optimist that I am and wanting every marriage to survive I delved in further about whether or not there existed any hope of reconciliation to which she replied, "I gave it a year. I tried. But the love never came back." She was shocked (likely she was really more irritated) when my unexpected response to her statement caught her off guard as it required a much more critical assessment of exactly what those words "I tried" really meant. My response simply queried:

"Well, what did you do?"

"Huh?"

"I mean, you said that you tried to fall back in love but it didn't work. I'm simply asking you what it was that you did or tried to do. What did you do in your attempt to make the love come back? Did you spend more time together? Did you go see a counselor? Did you start doing together the things you did when you first started dating and fell in love?"

While her irritation at my questioning was made apparent by her storming off and leaving my questions unanswered, it simply exemplified the point I was trying to make: that we often do nothing in our relationships, yet hope (or expect) for things to change. Poof, just like that! One day I was walking down the street and the "love fairy" decided that I should fall in love with Sam. So, totally outside of my power or control, fate (cupid, God, etc.) pierced me with his arrow and caused me to fall in love with him and I was overcome with these powerful feelings that proved to me that we were meant to be together forever.

But do we just know? Are we powerless to control this process of "falling in love" and when or with whom it happens? Or is there more to this phenomenon?

Well, let's just begin by considering that phrase "falling in love" as it tells us much more about our modern-day conception of love than we might at first glance realize. The word falling implies something accidental—something we have little control over. When we fall into a hole in the ground we are actually propelled forward by, in this case, the combination of gravity and some other force acting upon us such as our toes getting caught on a tree root grown above the ground in the sidewalk. Had we had the power to do so, we could have chosen to stop ourselves from falling and thus remained in our upright positions. But alas, we did not. We simply found ourselves mid-air for a split second, powerless to control what we knew was about to happen, and prayed that our lumbering, airborne bodies would find a forgiving landing.

Accordingly then, the statement that we *fall in love* implies much about our conception of that process of loving another. After our discussion about the changing definitions of the word "love" we now understand that language always seeks to do its best to find and use the best symbols possible to explain things, emotions, and situations. As such, our language changes, morphs, and grows as we gain new knowledge and mature.

Consider all the new words that have entered our vocabularies in the last several decades based on new knowledge and technology: "to Google" something has become a verb. The noun "snail mail" was borne out of the word that was previously simply called "mail" to differentiate between what we received through our "mailbox" and what we received through our "inbox." Think of the words sexting or e-blast (or e-anything) or the words "hooking up," which now represent the more casual nature of getting together with someone for little more than the recreational act of sex rather than the previously used words as "making love," which imply there was actual feeling involved in the sexual act. Or who could ever forget the notorious Miley Cyrus "incident" at the 2013 MTV Video Music Awards that introduced the word "twerking" into our vocabularies? I think I'd most certainly dislodge a vertebra if I were to attempt a twerking movement. I'll just leave that to the youthful Miss Cyrus. As stated earlier, the words we choose to represent these things present the clearest pictures possible of all other options to their users and hearers.

Returning then to the concept of "falling in love" we recognize the problematic nature of this ideology that signifies nothing more than merely the initial stages of a romantic relationship in which our brain's chemical makeup is temporarily altered by a powerful influx of "love" hormones. John Gottman calls this "The Physiology of Falling in Love Cocktail," which is the "magic" that happens when you meet the "right" person. According to Gottman, only some people can set off "the cascade of the falling in love cocktail in our body." So that's the first piece of good news for those whose marriages are struggling and tell themselves "I married the wrong person" or "we are simply incompatible" as I told myself for years when my own marriage was struggling. Apparently I was wrong. To a certain degree you are very physically compatible or you would never have been initially attracted in the first place. It just wouldn't have happened no matter how nice the guy or attractive the girl. This is also why many people who divorce end up marrying someone very much like their ex-spouse. The same type of person was needed to set off that cascade a second time as did the first time.

Among those eleven different hormones in the "love cocktail" that your body and mind are flooded with during these initial stages of a relationship are DHEA, which produces a natural amphetamine high; pheromones—sex scents—smell and attraction; oxytocin "the cuddle hormone" which, by the way, also reduces fear and good judgment (Go figure—the worst nightmare of every parent of hormonal teenagers); PEA, which spikes at ovulation and signals approach and romance; estrogen responsible for softness and receptivity; testosterone, which is responsible for aggressiveness, sexual desire and lust; serotonin responsible for emotional sensitivity and low irritability (Also one of my favorites. Ugh. *Nothing* they do while our serotonin is spiked will irritate us. *Everything* they do when it returns to normal does); dopamine—responsible for excitement, pleasure, motivation, and risk-taking (many an affair has begun because of this risk-taking influence of dopamine on lonely but otherwise happy or content spouses); progesterone, which is sedating, calming, and generally needs to be inhibited; prolactin, which reduces aggression and increases maternal nurturance; and, lastly, vasopressin, our monogamy molecule responsible for aggressive possessiveness in males. This spike in vasopressin makes it relatively impossible to be in love with two people at the same time which, in the case of infidelity, once we meet and start becoming attracted to someone new (not because we fell out of love with our spouse but rather let our guards down due to loneliness or drudgery [in most cases]) our spike in vasopressin will do its best to convince us we never loved our spouses in the first place. It's impossible for our monogamous brains to comprehend those beliefs because they are currently in high gear for a new individual who is paying significant attention to us. Phew. No wonder when we fall in love we fall hard.

For a time, when these hormones surge through our bodies we are literally "high" on love, we are fearless and thus take risks we wouldn't normally take if we were in our rational minds. We are less irritable so our future spouses see primarily our happy, agreeable, positive selves and very little of what our mates do irritates us like they most certainly will once this cocktail wears off ("Do you really have to chew your food so annoyingly?" "Why on earth do you have to ask so many questions? Can't you just get to the point?" "I am sick and tired of tripping on your shoes every time I walk in the front door."). Little, if anything, about our mates annoy us in this early stage and thus our mates feel encouraged by us (not criticized), proud to have us on their side, and thus our monogamy molecules help create in our future husbands an aggressive possessiveness of us, their women (desirousness of being only with her and protecting her from other males' attempts at gaining her affections—which is extremely attractive to women), therefore making their women feel as if they are the center of their husbands' world, which at this time they absolutely are.

I don't know about you but I remember extremely well the powerful attraction I felt for my husband when my body was flooded with this "love cocktail." I had been a nanny for a wonderful woman and her two sweet children—Rocky and Wesley. I had gotten the job because I filled in for a friend whose job it was and was going on a vacation for two weeks necessitating the fill-in. While there, I cleaned the house from top to bottom daily not because I was asked to but because it needed cleaning and I had fun doing it while caring for the children. We used to play all day or I'd engage in teaching them something like reading, etc. I loved teaching even back then at seventeen. After my two weeks were completed the parents asked me to stay on full time because they were so impressed with my attention to detail in all these areas. So for the next two summers this nanny job garnered nearly all of my daytime focus.

However, that all changed when I met my future husband and was flooded with the "love cocktail." Apparently, the mother began to grow concerned because after a month or so of my involvement with my sweetheart, she would come home to a less-than-spiffy house. Things were no longer maintained at my usual level of excellence, which, of course, was now the expected level. She was absolutely correct. I remember taking care of the children properly, but then, rather than clean as I used to, I would spend my remaining hours on the phone with my honey, or day dreaming about him, or writing him letters. I was quite embarrassed when this neglect of duties was brought to my attention. She probably would not have found it humorous if I had I told her I was unable to care properly for her children because I was high on a "love" cocktail.

Unfortunately, this cocktail eventually wears off and our hormonal levels return to normal. The "poor judgment haze" as Gottman calls it, produced by oxytocin, dopamine, and testosterone fades and our logic and judgment are re-activated. We begin to see our relationship and our partner in a more objective manner than we did during the initial stages of our relationship. This leveling takes, on average, two years. Bummer. Wouldn't everyone want this phase to last forever? Totally sucks. Or does it?

No one can question the extraordinarily pleasurable sensation of this initial relational stage. So much so that many find themselves continually moving on from one relationship to another once this stage has worn off in order to experience it again and again. Though as with any drug, the duration of this "high" from this "love cocktail" becomes shorter and shorter and more of it is then needed each and every time to achieve the original high. This is especially problematic if the person addicted to the "love cocktail" is already married or in a committed relationship as he or she often becomes a serial cheater. But I digress too much; it is much more fortunate for society and progress as a whole that this stage represents only a finite period of time. Should it not, and we remained perpetually in this stage, we would be so hyper-focused on spending time only with this other person that we would never leave the house. We would likely neglect all or most other areas of our lives such as our homes, our careers, and even our other family members. "Let's call in sick today so we can spend the day together." "I have a paper to write for my class. I really should be in the library, but I don't care. I would rather be here with you." It is literally impossible to remain fully rational during this hazy phase of love. Though it may not seem so at the time, this stage is an incredibly selfish stage of our relationships in the sense that we love how *we* feel while we are with the other. Though it may seem I want to stay in this phase because of my focus on the other person, the true pleasure I wish to maintain are the pleasurable feelings being with that person brings to me.

Further, if "the two are to become one" it becomes one's primary responsibility to help the other to recognize and minimize his or her weaknesses in order that they become better versions of themselves. This would clearly not take place while on a love "high" as we are necessarily blinded to our mate's weaknesses. (You'll gain a better understanding of this in the chapter on perception). I am sure you get the picture at this point. It's great while it lasts but, unfortunately, what goes up does in fact naturally have to come back down. So what once took place effortlessly and painlessly (love) must now, if we are to remain "in love" become a conscious *choice* and must now take place much more deliberately—even for Super Couples.

So let me say it right now: Love is *not* a feeling. Love is that which makes the feelings arrive—love me first and the feelings will follow.

Hmm...well, if love isn't necessarily a feeling and we don't actually "fall" into it, what then *is* love and what causes us "to love" another?

Simply put—love is an action.

LOVE AS AN ACTION
LOVE BURNS CALORIES...

Love is something we *do*. If we once before *chose* to love another human being, it is wholly possible to choose to love that same human being a second time, and a third, and a fourth... or daily...or even forever. Let me share with you a story to help explain.

I used to work with a man named Carl. When I first met Carl, he began to talk about this woman, who was a relatively well-known and acclaimed opera singer. We were planning an event and he talked about how awesome she was and how we should get her to perform at our event in order to attract audiences. He was quite persistent. Every time I heard him speak in a professional setting he always seemed to find some way to introduce Patty's name into the conversation as if it were killing him to go too long without talking about this woman. But Carl is a private man and thus it took me nearly a year later to realize that this singer was his ex-wife, that he and she had struck up a new and improved relationship and they were beginning to date again. Another year passed and I bumped into Carl again whereupon I discovered that he and his ex-wife were now newlyweds again. When questioned about their relationship he blushed and smiled from ear to ear like most any other young couple wed for the first time.

So what happened? How could two people who once shared so much disdain for one another that they chose to divorce rather than to have to look at, talk to, or live with each other, all of a sudden desire to be in each other's lives so intimately that they wanted to remarry and share every moment of every day with each other? Did the gods of love and fate decide to play some kind of sick joke on these two lovers by causing them to fall into love, out of love, and then back into love again—beyond their own control—like two puppets on a fateful tether? Well, if one adheres to the concept of soul mates being destined one for the other then this concept would seem to hold some credence. They just got lucky, and then unlucky, and then lucky again. Phew! Quite the prankster that little guy Cupid!

Patty and Carl married at twenty and twenty-three respectively and felt blessed beyond imagination. However, three short years later they divorced. What happened to turn them from "I can't wait to spend every single day for the rest of my life with you" to "I no longer can stand to be in the same house as you?" Did each of them change and become "different" people as so many of us claim when we leave our spouses? Or did their perceptions change? Now, so many years have passed neither of them is able to recall with clarity what exactly it was they were saying to each other and how they were saying it (which is probably good), but they are clearly now seeing and saying things differently. Undoubtedly, there is a great respect for one another. They esteem the other in ways they likely did not before, or took for granted. Three years after they remarried I sat in Carl's office to discuss some business issues and he regularly found ways to mention how talented his wife was and just how good she was and how she's traveled the world because of her beautiful voice. His esteem for her was clearly evident. Further, to look at the two of them gushing when they interact is to think they are again schoolchildren in love. But they are not. They are in their sixties and had been divorced for nearly four decades before they began, once again, to communicate on a more loving and respectful manner—they began to reconnect.

When we first meet our spouses something is taking place— action. Words that are said, looks that are given, actions that take place, such as doors being held, flowers being purchased, cards being sent, time being spent with us, listening, laughing, sharing, playing, discussing, etc.

When my husband and I first got together I went with him to a car show and a boat show. I went camping with him in the cold, dark, scary forest (with nary a blow dryer, electrical outlet, or tube of lipstick to be found.) No matter what it was, if he invited me I said "Yes!" But likewise, Dan went with me to the mall, to my favorite nightclub where I loved to dance, and, worse yet, to the Prom. He hates the Prom! My husband hates dancing, hates crowds, hates noise (unless it's the revving of a loud engine blowing carbon—I learned that from him––that was the noise that turned him on) and my husband can't *stand* being the center of attention. What makes this all the more charmingly painful for him is that I was crowned Prom Princess, which meant Dan had to dance with me under a spotlight in front of 200 people he did not know, at a venue at which he did not want to be, and all the while wearing a tuxedo he did not want to wear with cameras photographing the event lest he somehow bury it way too deep in the recesses of his brain to ever have to retrieve it.

I bring this up to magnify one extremely important component of "falling in," "falling out," or staying in love. We begin *to love* those *whose actions* make us *feel* good. Their actions make us feel loved, or respected, or appreciated or in some way—the center of their world. Dan's actions that day (and weeks leading up to it) were all about me. Every single action evidenced the fact that I had been on his mind consistently "What color is your dress?" (He needed to order just the perfect bouquet to match). "I have planned a surprise for you next week." (Wow, a significant portion of his brain space and time had been devoted to *me. How incredibly attractive)*. These were clearly actions that my young lover undertook on my account. He did something *for me*. As a result I *felt* absolutely loved. Dan wasn't thinking about hunting, or work, or the Packers. He was thinking about *me*! His *actions* confirmed that I was the center of his world and I loved it.

I saw a TV show today that featured a rock star on stage. Around her perimeter were thousands of adoring fans looking up at her, screaming her name, trying to touch her, smiling because they got to be closer to her than did any others and, from its appearance, most would have sacrificed their right arms to get on stage and actually touch her.

How do you think this woman felt being adored by thousands of fans? Pretty good I would think. Yet, I'm certain she still had her needs for privacy, quiet time, and any other activity she chooses to do alone or with a chosen few loved ones. If you asked this rock star if she felt loved, desired, pretty, talented, envied, or whatever positive emotions one can think of in these moments, she'd likely say "unquestionably, yes." Now don't get too sidetracked thinking, "Well, I'd hate to be on stage or the center of attention," as my husband would definitely say. That's not the point. The point is, we humans desire to be loved, are designed to be loved and our selfish human nature would be much more comforted knowing we are loved, desired, and esteemed in some way than it would if it felt lonely, unloved, unappreciated, and unnoticed. Through the actions of those many others making her the center of their world for that time, this woman on stage received their by-product of good feelings. And those feelings are intoxicating.

So what about that newlywed couple at the baseball game at the beginning of this chapter? All couples experience some good feelings at the onset of their relationship or they wouldn't have married. (So did you, even if you've since forgotten or don't want to admit it because you are currently in a troubled relationship.) Clearly, this couple was experiencing some loving feelings too, because at that moment he was making her the center of his world. But does he do this all the time and will they constantly love one another? Do they sometimes experience moments of unloving behaviors too? By the looks on their faces and the tears shed the couple was experiencing some very loving feelings as they stood in front of the stadium full of onlookers. Most would agree this couple was "in love" at that time. And it is very likely there were numerous onlookers wishing they were as "in love" as that embracing couple. I would have had those thoughts during my troubled years. Actually I had them regularly. I'd think, "Now *that* couple is in love. I wish my husband would love me like that." And I still do. That would be a great way for my husband to love me on a given day.

There is nothing wrong with wanting to be loved and

allowing others' actions toward their spouse to influence our equally loving actions towards ours. As a matter of fact, for a thriving, long-term marriage it is essential to practice loving actions daily. The problem occurs not when we *desire* loving actions but when we *idealize* other couples as if their love were a bit more effortless than most. Did you idealize *that* couple? Would your opinions change if you knew this husband had just left his wife and three young children for this woman and that this relationship was the product of his sixth affair? Now what do you think about their love? Does he *love* his new wife or is he simply exhibiting momentary loving actions?

As you can now see, loving feelings come and go proportionality with loving actions. This husband once "loved" his first wife and likely showed his love to her. But over time, as his loving actions decreased, so too, did his loving feelings for her and hers for him. I am confident this man "loves" his young wife much more frequently now than he will ten years from now when "the love cocktail" has long since dissipated and life, work, kids, bills, step-kids, ex-wives, and all the accompanying "baggage" begin to take up more of their attention. If he neglects his duty *to love* her daily—through thoughtful, loving, wife-centered actions—then, just as in his first marriage, her loving feelings for him will likewise dissipate. But I'm an optimist. People learn. I learned and so can you. Love takes calories. You need to burn more than a few to get to super in your marriage. As such, in this next chapter we are going to redefine love. We will then teach you how to maintain that love.

REDEFINING LOVE

As this chapter has thoroughly asserted, if we are to stay "in love" forever, we must continue to work "to love" forever. We must separate feelings from actions. I am definitely not a stoic— far from it. Rather, I am likely one of the greatest romantics that has ever walked this earth. I am passionate, emotional, tender yet strong. I am sensual. I love feeling loved and desired, cared for, and esteemed. Mostly, I desire to experience not only an extremely happy marriage but one that is accompanied by the deepest feelings for and romantic expressions from my lover that constantly remind me I am the center of his world. I want to be the girl being surprised at the stadium or sent love notes for no reason, or told I am the most amazing woman God ever created and I want to be told in front of male and female friends and strangers alike by a husband who unabashedly desires to profess his love for me like a leading man to his leading lady on the silver screen. I desire to dance alone in our candlelit living room to a love song that reminds us that our love is still strong and a priority. I want roses. I want surprises. I want my husband's heart...or at least proof that I already have it. I want it all. I want the fairytale.

Super Couple marriages, though imperfect, are filled with actions like the man above who expressed his love to his wife in deed. It was a moment of time that brought happiness for well... that moment. He had to put forth effort to plan for that moment and to orchestrate all that was necessary to pull off such a big feat. The problems arise when the effort is no longer expended each day, week, month, or year throughout their lifetime and the spouse thus at some point in time is no longer central in his thoughts—as made known through his deeds—or lack thereof. But in that moment she was made to feel the center of his world and that centrality made her feel loved. This is an area in which Super Spouses excel. So let's take a closer look at this principle.

I WANT TO BE THE CENTER OF HIS/HER WORLD!

Spousal centrality is that which makes Super Couples...well, super. When couples fall in love I always say that they don't fall in love with another person as much as they fall in love with the feeling of being the center of that person's world. As we've already discussed, were this not true, "falling in love" seemingly would be accidental, something we'd have no control over and thus, would also mean we'd have no control over falling *out of love* either. The massive cultural changes of the late twentieth century that changed our understanding of love, commitment, and marriage are partially responsible for the ideology that declared *"You deserve to be happy. If your spouse no longer makes you happy, you're doing no one any good—not even your children. So get out, cut your losses, and better luck next time.*" Additionally, this is the forefather of the current ideology that proposes the concept of a soul mate—the idea that of the billions of people alive there is only one person alone compatible with and destined to be with another. While I will address this notion in a later chapter, I am certain you may be scratching your head thinking, "Well, Christine, isn't that what Super Couples are anyway—perfectly made for one another alone forever?" I must clarify that the current concept of soul mate must be tweaked as it dangerously presumes "soul mate" to be intrinsic and effortless and that once found requires minimal effort to remain "in love" forevermore. This research has revealed "Super" requires daily effort and effort creates soul mates. Thus all of these mantras, though well intended, are missing the ideological mark. Super Couples are deliberate in keeping their spouses at the center of their lives.

When we are born we are all, by nature, selfish. From the first moments we enter the world we scream and expect someone to tend to our needs and, for the most part, they do. I'm hungry. Feed me! I'm lonely. Hold me! I'm wet. Change me! I'm tired, let me sleep. Fortunately, for most human beings these cries are immediately responded to by another who soothes those pleas by meeting our needs—and doing so quickly, fully, and lovingly. Further, as we grow from infant to toddler and toddler to child the idea that we actually *are* the center of someone's world is reinforced every time we are applauded or approved: "Oh, look at momma's pretty girl! You're daddy's little princess! Such a handsome boy! I'm so proud of you! You went potty all by yourself! Of course you can be an astronaut! You're the smartest girl in the whole wide world!" And consider how quickly we run to our child when they are hurt or fall down and scrape their knee. We'll have a Super Hero Band-Aid on that knee before the nerve ending even completes its split-second journey to the brain. We begin our lives actually *being* the center of someone else's world and we like it. It's intoxicating. We feel loved. We feel contented. We are at peace. Our needs are met and we are happy. It really is "all about me" at this point—until a sibling comes along, that is, and we lose our solitary role as the axis of our parents' world and are forced to share the spotlight and the attention. However, even within this sharing of attention we can still be happy knowing that when we call someone answers—lovingly—as they love us so much they would do anything to see us succeed. Even without younger siblings this transition from "center of my world" still takes place, though at a much different pace and set of experiences.

As we grow, and if we do so in a relationally healthy environment, we learn that we are not necessarily the center of anyone's world (though we never lose the desire to be). We learn to self-soothe and do what it takes to meet our own needs. We learn to become independent. We become self-centered—out of necessity for the most part—but self-centered nonetheless. For instance, we learn to feed ourselves (if we don't, who will?). We play with the people that *we* enjoy being around. We participate in the sports that *we* enjoy playing. We take jobs or seek college majors that suit *our* needs. Basically, we begin to establish our own identities and discover those things that make us happiest. As an adult, I have learned that I need seven hours of uninterrupted sleep each night, and so I ensure I get my seven hours. I've learned I don't feel good physically or psychologically unless I get in a good run or a workout every morning so I schedule exercise into my day. When I'm hungry I eat because I want to sate the hunger. Basically, we all have needs that must be met in order to make us happy and, for the most part, we prioritize getting our own needs met (unless we have small children where that priority necessarily becomes secondary). Many of those needs we aren't even aware of and can't articulate, though they create a yearning within us that will not cease until that need is somehow met. And as we enter our journey of self-discovery we become independent of others, including our primary care-givers, and seek to go out into the world to not only discover but meet our unique physical, emotional, spiritual, intellectual, and relational needs.

Within our search for independence ironically, we are searching for others with whom to share our life's journeys, someone with whom we can count on to do those things *we wish to do* with us. I am not talking about our romantic relationships yet, but simply our friendships. Consider our earlier discussion about extraverts and introverts. Temperament research has shown we tend to hang out with those whose personalities are most like our own and who like to do the same things as do we.

If we are both the same we won't have to worry about whose needs to meet because we'll be meeting the needs of both most of the time. Though there will arise the occasions where I may not want to do the same thing as my friend Cheryl, I am willing to do so because there have been times when she, too, sacrificed her needs for me. But the amount of time we disagree and have to do something we would prefer not to do is minimal. It's a minor sacrifice. Friendships are friendships because they are easy. When they become too much work we walk. So while our friendships aren't overtly self-centered or selfish, it exemplifies that we don't have to be especially selfless either.

Let's consider, however, a time when my friends want to go shopping, fishing, or some other activity and I want to go to the movies or stay home. My options on these days are to either submit my needs to theirs, thereby being relatively selfless, or we each do as we wish thereby each focusing on her own needs. On these occasions we likely go our separate ways for the day. Now I'm not saying this latter option is especially selfish in the sense that is usually negatively connoted by the word "selfish" because we all need our "me" time. But in the purest sense of the word we are both reverting to meeting the needs of the self rather than the needs of the other, which is, essentially, selfishness. What allows this to take place in platonic relationships with few negative impacts is that there exist different expectations for friendships than for monogamous, committed, and loving relationships. I don't *expect* all of my girlfriends to meet all of my needs nor do they expect me to meet theirs. That's why we have more than one friend. A different friend meets a different need at a different time. While we love each other and want to see each other happy, we also realize we are not solely responsible for the other's happiness. We simply contribute to it as often as is convenient for us without extraordinary efforts. We are not the center of each other's worlds and we know it. Thus, we have lower expectations of our friends than we do of our spouses. For that reason, I'm extremely happy when my girlfriends and family members do something for my benefit. They did so even though I realized that they didn't *have to*.

My family and friends recently threw me a fiftieth birthday party. It was awesome. It took a lot of time, talent, planning, and money and yet all those involved sacrificed some of that just for me—to make me happy. They met my need for love and attention on that day. They made me the center of their world. But they all have lives and families and needs of their own. For those reasons, none could possibly be expected to make me the center of their world each subsequent day as well. That would be extremely unrealistic of me to assume, and I can't make all of them the center of my world all of the time either—at different moments of time, yes, but not daily. As such, the rarity of these days make them all the more special to their recipients.

While the scenarios mentioned above (the need to go shopping, to the movies, or hang out) occur within romantic relationships as well, in friendship there is little to no pressure involved because we are not exclusively committed to our friends as we would be to our lovers or spouses in monogamous relationships. They have other friends and social circles apart from the ones in which we share, as do I, and on those days where our needs don't match we hang out with those other friends whose needs meet our own that day—little to no submission required. Further, if I have a particular friend who infrequently if ever meets my needs or seeks to do so, over time that person and I will simply cease to be close friends. We will move on because the friendship is no longer serving any purpose—there is no legal or emotional commitment requiring us to stay in the friendship and thus we move on to relationships that *do* meet our needs. To summarize, the previous discourse was simply aimed at illuminating the selfish nature of all human beings—*all humans*. Existence necessitates a basic level of selfishness.

I have many friends. When Cheryl can't meet my need I call Amy or Crystal or Kisha or whoever will best meet that particular need. I get to pick between them and thus the need almost always gets met because one of them is going to be good at whatever it is that I need at that time and vice versa. Having all of our needs met is harder to do within a marriage however when all of one's expectations are put onto one imperfect person. It's impossible for Dan to meet all of my psychological, emotional, financial, and physiological needs. Often the greatest reason we "fall in love" with someone is because we do, in fact, feel as if we are the center of their world—as they have just become the center of ours and they seemingly are meeting all or most of our needs at that time.

When we meet those persons we love romantically, something unnatural happens. All of a sudden we go from being self-centered to being other-centered (albeit temporarily). While to a substantially lesser degree this also takes place in some of our platonic relationships where the newness allows us to temporarily place another on a metaphorical pedestal, the focus here will be on the romantic relationship wherein this pattern is relatively ubiquitous.

Consider the first time we meet that special "other" (regardless of whether this one ultimately ends up being our spouse). The initial stages of most any romantic relationship follow this predictable pattern. For those with whom we are most compatible this pattern is sustained for a much longer period of time than with those with whom we eventually break up, which is why we decide this one is "special" and worth marrying.

As we've already discussed the initial stages of romantic relationships, our primary concern here is to reiterate that in this stage where we are hyper-focused on thoughts of the other we are submitting our own needs to the needs of the other and making them the center of our world. We are overwhelmed by thoughts of and pleasant feelings for this person. When you set a date you remain hypersensitive to every detail leading to the date. You pay extra attention to your hair, face, and clothing not because you are *self*-focused per se, but precisely the opposite: you are so *other*-focused you make an unnaturally concentrated effort on self-presentation to please the other. You clean out your car and vacuum the food fragments that had otherwise been fermenting into fossil fuel since two presidents prior—the same food fragments you hadn't even noticed until you realized this person would be sitting in your passenger seat. Now you notice. You pay keener attention to details that, prior to meeting this person, went unnoticed or you were apathetic to. All of a sudden every detail of your appearance matters. (Every mother of teen males in this stage appreciates this sudden obsession with the opposite sex as his previously godforsaken hygiene finally matters to him and he bathes.) The appearance of your apartment, your car, and your body matter. You smile more. You eat less. You lose weight because instead of food occupying your brain space there is now something—or *someone*—better in its place. You get the picture. In this beginning phase we are one hundred percent focused on another to the negation of our own needs. In this stage we are unnaturally *selfless*.

I'd like to share an example from a young man who attended one of my pre-marital seminars. We were discussing this very principle when he said:

> When my fiancé and I first started dating we were in high school. During her senior year, after I had graduated and taken a job, I missed seeing her every day and bumping into her in the halls between classes. Our time together was never enough—no matter how many hours we had been together in a given week, I always wanted more. My girlfriend was on the high school dance team and I knew that every day at precisely 12:15 she would be practicing on the stage in the auditorium. I planned my lunches around her schedule. All morning as I worked all I did was look at the clock, which seemed to move at a snail's pace. At precisely noon I would run to the time clock and immediately head to her school. It took me twenty minutes to get there. I would skip my lunch (because food wasn't allowed in the auditorium), sit in the back of the room, and watch her dance. I'd stay the twenty minutes I could before having to race back to work to clock back in with few minutes to spare. Those twenty minutes we were within eyeshot of each other flew but they were the best minutes of my day. We didn't even talk but she knew I was there and that was all it took to make us both smile.

As this young man recalled this story, his fiancé's face lit up as she, too, recalled the feelings generated by her young lover's uninhibited and hyper-focused attention on her—on making her the center of his world. She reached under the table and grabbed his hand. The actions came first and the feelings followed.

In this example, the young suitor negated his own needs in order to meet the needs of his love interest. Of course seeing her was also meeting his mutual need but the focus of this example is the fact that he willingly negated his own needs to please his sweetheart. I would argue again that this young lady didn't fall in love with this young man as much as she fell in love with being at the center of his world. It appealed greatly to her needs to be loved and desired. Had this young man not pursued her with such attention she likely may not have fallen in love with him.

When I first met my husband I worked at Baskin-Robbins. Each day worked I was allowed two free scoops of ice cream. I looked forward to that reward daily. When my young suitor visited me the first time, he ordered two scoops of French Vanilla. I handed them to him free of charge—I had given him *my* free scoops (and they were significantly larger than the two and a half ounce scoops I was trained to serve). I willingly sacrificed my own wants to meet his. It brought me great pleasure to do so too. Further, the idea of it being a sacrifice didn't even cross my mind. To me, like most in this initial relational stage, we would spend a majority of our minutes, hours, and days considering different and frequent options to please our lovers. These gestures did not have to be grand or expensive either. They could have been the most simple of gestures and yet their impact was powerful and memorable because the sincerity of the gesture was palpable. For me, I would now bring home French Vanilla as often as my young budget allowed. I would bring home larger quantities—proof that I actually spent money to please him—rather than bringing the two scoops I got for free.

In the same vein, Dan missed few opportunities to please me as well. I recall once in our first year of marriage while driving together when Dan pulled the car into the parking lot of our local grocery store and told me he needed to run in for something he'd forgotten. Five minutes later he returned with nothing but a bouquet of flowers and handed them to me. This was it? He had forgotten nothing at all? He simply sought an excuse to please me—because he knew I loved not only flowers but also spontaneity and surprise. Then again, maybe he didn't know this yet. More likely, as is the case with most, it made Dan feel good to make me feel good. Now, thirty years later as I recall this loving gesture I still smile as this long-ago formed memory has never, ever, left. It was and still is so emotionally pleasurable that it has impressed itself into my brain's memory center. And it will never leave me. Ever.

Our gestures in this stage do not have to be expensive or cost anything at all. You realize he is just too busy getting ready for a big inspection, exam, or business meeting and you take his car to the car wash without him realizing it because you know how much he loves his car. You have no problem whatsoever performing this service for him because it makes you feel good to make him feel good—to please him and meet his needs. You text her for no reason in the middle of the day to let her know you are thinking about her. You go to her scrapbooking convention, or gun show, or car show because you know this is something your lover enjoys and, after all, all you want to do is please her, watch her smile, make him happy.

Nothing more.

Nothing less.

Because you love him/her.

So why are these experiences so powerful? So memorable? Were the flowers my husband bought me back in 1983 really *that* important that I will forever remember them? Were they especially rare or expensive? Absolutely not. As a matter of fact I remember nothing at all about the flowers except they were the inexpensive kind that sits in a water bucket at the store's entrance. You know, the kind that are held together by a rubber band and plastic wrap and sold for a nominal price of $9.99 or so. None of this mattered to me then nor matters now. The part of the event that caused it to be seared into my memory was that *I,* not the flowers, was so important to my young husband that I held a central part of his brain space. He was thinking about *me.* He was focused on *me—*on *pleasing me.* While driving together that day so many years ago Dan was not thinking of hunting or football or work or bills or anything else, but only of me. His actions proved I was not only on his mind in a meaningful way but that he loved me and wanted to please me so much so that he thought of a way to prove it to me. At that moment, I felt as if I was the center of his world. And *this* is what I fell in love with—what we all fall in love with. And it felt good.

The chemicals and hormones our bodies produce during this early stage as a result of these reciprocal kindnesses and attention are powerful. They are so strong that we associate these feelings with the person performing the actions as if the person were the cause of the feelings. Now hear me out, associating one's spouse with great feelings is not a bad thing. As I said earlier, I am a hopeless romantic and have no problem whatsoever seeing my husband as wholly good and awesome and the cause of my warm heart. After all, this is ultimately the goal of each of us and the goal of this book: to be extremely happy with our mates—Super Couples. The problem occurs when we detach the actions of the person from those positive feelings and associate them merely with the existence of the other. "I feel good when Danny stands next to me, so I must love him."

But consider this. What if all of a sudden that same person hits me across my face, calls me a horrible name, disrespects me, insults me, or does something I consider extremely unpleasant? Would I still have those same loving feelings? Of course not. Not only would the good and loving feelings disappear within a nanosecond they would also and immediately be replaced with equally powerful negative feelings of disgust, anger, bewilderment, or stunned disillusionment. My example may have been drastic but I wanted to ensure I used a scenario certain to elicit the desired emotions. Point made. We fall in love with one's actions toward us and those actions produce feelings. Our society's marriages are falling apart because somehow we have forgotten this pattern and disassociated actions from feelings and attached them rather to persons.

It is this same principle that is partially responsible for the increase of marriages affected or destroyed by infidelity. My spouse stops *doing* things that please me or that let me know I was on his mind, let alone the center of his world. Even if I am unconscious of this relational void at a given time (because I'm busy with kids, school, work, building a new house, or just living life) I, too, am likely doing nothing to maintain this other-centeredness, let alone doing anything to rekindle associated feelings. In this stage we are again beginning to focus primarily on the self. Whether accidental or intentional, the self-centeredness cannot be negated—and the feelings follow. Sadly, in many cases, someone else (who is not even attempting to pursue you at first) comes into the picture who begins to meet your needs—needs that you hadn't even consciously realized were unmet until they were being met again. This person tries to please you (because that's just the type of person he/she is) by doing kind and thoughtful things for you, or spending time with you, or making you laugh, or finding an interest in things you have an interest in and those feelings begin to rear their little heads again—not yet the romantic feelings, but simply the pleasurable feelings associated with being thought of by another person. So we start doing more stuff with that person—because it feels good. Over time, we begin to find ways to spend more time with this person to whom (for the sake of my example) you are not even yet cognizant of your attraction. Eventually, you are spending more and more time with this other person and less and less time with your spouse. Consequently, your positive feelings for this person begin to grow, deepen, and become more frequent while your positive feelings with your spouse, mate, fiancé begin to fade, weaken, and become less frequent. How could they not? Remember the monogamy molecule? Since your spouse is no longer the central focus of your thoughts, actions and attention, the associated positive feelings also no longer exist.

And we all know what happens next. The feelings for the other become so overwhelming that we eventually come to a decision point. We realize we feel good when with the lover and bad or apathetic when with the spouse. We have "fallen out of love." Too many relationships have followed this very predictable pattern. Millions of relationships have, over time, done so, maybe even yours. And it sucks. It sucks because now we must decide our ultimate fate: "Do I want to stay with my mate with whom I've built a family, share friends, a home, a checkbook, a dog, a life, and for whom I no longer have any feelings, or do I want to go to my lover with whom I share all these magnificent feelings and begin anew?" (Remember the risk-taking hormone and the one that minimizes irritability? Who cares if we will have to separate and share our kids, our budgets, and our property? This *feels* so right. The kids will adapt and we'll make it work.) At this point no easy option exists. No matter which way you turn you will experience some form of extreme pain and grief associated with loss. If you choose the lover and the current yet temporary euphoric feelings, you will be forced to grieve the family, the history, a portion of the esteem and respect others had for you (because a small amount of this respect *will* in fact be lost—

to include a part of our self-esteem and all the self-doubts associated with divorce—*"Can I ever trust myself again to make a right decision?"*) and, you will definitely grieve part of your budget and material lifestyle. This holds true regardless if one is the leaver or the one being left. Paradoxically, if you decide to leave the lover you will experience a great and devastatingly painful (but also temporary) loss of those euphoric feelings. You will grieve the idyllic and unrealistic life you had imagined— though its attainment is highly unlikely and irrational (the same one you likely imagined when you first met your spouse but have since forgotten). And it will hurt. Badly.

Though it may appear the focus of this chapter has digressed, it has not. It has simply shown how our focus forges our feelings. Like with vision, we can focus only on that which we place at the center of our gaze. Everything else, though still visible, is relegated to the periphery. I can stare at a garden, but if I desire to know it better, become more intimate with all of its intricacies I must draw closer to it, and look at it one flower at a time. To smell its pleasing fragrance I must place my face closer to its blossoms and inhale deeply. I must touch it. I must actively seek to learn about it. What kind of flowers are these? Do they need full sun or partial shade? How much water does this garden require? When should I prune it and how? You see, if I am focused deeply on one garden it is impossible for me to focus equally as deeply on another garden. And once I've decided on which garden to focus I cannot ever expect that garden to grow unless I daily force myself to study its flowers because each day a new flower appears, dies, or is infected with some annoying little pest that— if left untreated—will destroy the entire garden. I may be initially interested in the roses but over time I may discover that in the garden there are also hyacinths and daylilies and realize they, too, have a wholly unique but beautiful fragrance. But you'd have never discovered them had you stared only at the roses. Stare closely enough too and you'll occasionally find a weed or two. You won't like them and will have to pluck them once discovered. But if you keep your focus on the entire garden it will never become overgrown with the weeds but rather the flowers.

My experience writing this book can be used as another example of the aforementioned principle. I'd been saying I wanted to get this book completed for almost four years now and on occasion I would sit and write it...for a couple hours. But then I would have to stop to do my day job. And then I needed to spend time with my grandchildren, or my girlfriends, and then I needed to focus on my seminars, oh and don't forget I needed to spend time with my Super-husband-to-be. Though all of these responsibilities necessarily needed a portion of my time, every minute I spent doing something besides writing was one where my focus shifted off the book and it stopped getting written. I had valid excuses for why other things took priority. But it still remains that I could only focus on one thing at a time, and the book was being neglected. The funny thing is that over time, I also noticed there was never a shortage of things to take my focus off of my writing and so I had to make a conscious decision: 2000 words a week needed to be written in order to be completed by my deadline. I started to spend more days in the library and I knew I would complete fewer projects outside the library. It's just the way things had to be. My house was no longer as compulsively cleaned as before. I could only spend one night a week with my grandchildren instead of three, or I'd spend two-hour blocks with them and not eight. I'd have to write rather than help my husband paint (big sacrifice there), or only exercise one hour a day instead of two or run two out of town races instead of six. I'd give up time in front of the TV or listening to music or...

My focus had to shift and the book had to become my priority in order to achieve my goal of publication. But a really cool thing began to happen. Instead of dreading the time sacrifice in order to lock myself in the library where my only friends were my laptop and my latte, I began to see progress as the book grew from an outline to several pages, and then to chapters. Eventually the book took shape and the thought of spending time alone with it began to excite me. As a matter of fact I couldn't wait to get to the library today because of the positive feelings I've begun to experience on this project of love (the opposite of what was happening when not giving it focused attention). I began to see not how many pages I lacked but how many had been written and how few remained until completion. We were growing together.

Like a personal relationship, I saw my devoted attention was paying off and it became a joy. The book-writing process taught me I could not have my cake and eat it too. In my ideal world, I could have my grandbabies five days a week, run as many races as I wanted, spend every waking hour with my husband and still get the book done in record time. But we don't live in an ideal world. We only have so many hours in a day and we need to put those things and relationships that are our greatest priority in first and second positions respectively. So what is your priority?

Career, Children, and Other Subverters

Before I move from this topic of priorities, I'd like to add two more factors that commonly contribute to our misalignment of priorities: children and careers. Women often make children the center of their world and many men place career and "significance" at the center of theirs. Regardless of gender, what is imperative is that in both examples the spouse is no longer central.

I wish to illuminate the insidious threat to Superness that each of these can be. If you are anything like me you may be thinking "Well of course my children are my first priority. They *need* me and cannot survive without me. My spouse can." While it is unquestionable that our children's basic needs must be a priority for both parents, their relational needs—your relationship with them—must be second to your relationship with your spouse. Numerous marriage and family experts have agreed the best gift you can give your children is to love their other parent. In this sense we mean providing our children with their basic physiological needs but also their needs for emotional security as well. *Watching mommy and daddy love one another makes me feel so secure in my own life that I can focus on being a kid.*

For twenty years I maintained the rationale that if I were in a sinking boat and I could only save my spouse or my children I'd undoubtedly save my children. And why wouldn't I? Looking back, my children made me much happier than did my spouse. Or was it that I focused more attention on my children than my spouse (thus relegating him to a non-central position in my thoughts and actions) that resulted in my closer relationship with my kids? I didn't fight with my children. (For the sake of this illustration, let's just skip past those attitude-ridden teen years when I actually wanted to throw them over the boat.) I had fun with them, we went to events together, and they adored me. At the end of their days it was me who they came home to, shared their hurts with, and trusted to make things better. Summed up: my children made me feel as if I was the center of their world and it felt good. The above example does not refer to the excessive hovering of helicopter parents but rather that there were no conditions to their love for me, nor mine for them. Thus those relationships were nurtured. The one with my spouse, sadly, was not, though neither of us realized it.

A priority is defined as "higher in importance, rank or privilege." As with our money when we place spending as a higher priority over saving or vice versa, we realize we can't both save and spend without dividing our resources between our financial priorities. If we are saving for a house we focus, for a time, on saving for that house. We eat Ramen noodles more often in order to deposit more into the house fund. Once purchased, we can reassess our priorities and reallocate our resources. Relationships work the same way. The ones we nurture grow and the ones we neglect perish. If our spouses are no longer our relational priorities—higher in importance than our children—our marriages will perish.

The arrival of children unquestionably demands a significant reallocation of emotional resources. Super Couples, however, make a deliberate effort to maintain proper *balance* between spousal and parental relationships. Super Couples *always* place their spousal relationship above that of their children—thus fostering thriving relationships with their children as well. Now remember, not even Super Spouses are perfect. I must ensure they remain off of the metaphorical marriage pedestal many of us place them on to our own detriment. They are still imperfect people who are *deliberate* in making their marital relationships their top priority in their lives.

When asked the "Whom would you save first?" question, each Super Spouse struggled to answer. For them it wasn't as easy as it was for me and many other couples. Some said they'd choose their spouse "because you could always have more children" and some chose their spouse "because they would grab the arms of the children too" but none said they'd choose their children above their spouses unless they felt it's what their spouse would want them to do (again trying to please the spouse first). Though the above scenario was only hypothetical, the Super Couples interviewed all revealed a more concrete proof that they made their spouses their first relational priorities. They did so through date nights and childless vacations.

Date nights? Couples' vacations? Wow! Now there's a concept. As I write, I still seem to shake my head at my apparent ignorance of what now seems common sense. Sadly, I have learned I am not alone in this ignorance as so many other couples likewise neglect the imperative of maintaining a healthy dating life throughout married life. It was so effortless in the early years that we take for granted the relational building and maintenance that takes place through spending quality and quantity time with each other. Super Couples protect this part of their relationships passionately. And why? Remember, actions produce feelings. Super Couples want to ensure those feelings never depart.

Every night when Duane would arrive home from a long day at work, he and Gina would send the children to their rooms and spend their first hour together in the living room discussing their day—often over a glass of wine. They advised that during this time the children knew they were not to bother their parents or interrupt this nightly ritual. This time devoted to one another was to Gina and Duane, sacred. While they would not have characterized this as a date per se, in essence this is what it was. What their children saw modeled was the centrality of the spousal relationship. Practices like this, research has shown, do not scar the children (though they will still vie for parent attention) but rather, provide the children with an emotionally secure environment.

Gina and Duane weren't alone in their deliberate "dating" either. Tricia and Jim, the youngest Super Couple interviewed and early into their childrearing years with four children under the age of eight, also protect their date nights. While they admit they go out less frequently than they would like, they do go out at least once a month to recharge their relationship and stay connected. Of course, said Tricia, "We spend most of our time discussing the children while out" but that, they say is unimportant. The fact that they are able to do so uninterrupted by some kind of preschool drama is all it takes to remind them why they fell in love with one another. Further, Tricia and Jim plan at least one childless vacation a year to nourish their relationship. And by the looks of it to this outside observer, it was working.

Without chronicling the responses of every couple, it should be known these two couples represent one hundred percent of the couples interviewed. Each sought to keep their marital relationship central and did so deliberately through time alone with their spouse. They made each other a priority even when it wasn't easy to do so.

During our troubled years, Dan and I never made dating a priority. We may have gone out on occasion with another couple or group, but it was extremely infrequent. Searching my marital archives I must admit I have zero memories of date nights where the two of us got a babysitter and went out alone. None. Not one memory. I will take much of the responsibility as, on my part, I didn't recall desiring to do so. Based on poor communication that had us speaking in improper and ugly tones (causing near daily fights) the last thing I desired was time alone with this person who brought me no happiness. However, poor communication aside, I now see how my devoted attention to our children allowed me to place them in priority position as the "center of my world."

While for some, children are a first priority, for others it's career. More often this is true of husbands. Some focus so much on their desire to provide that they neglect nurturing the relationships; the career becomes central. Worse, the family becomes secondary and the marriage a tertiary priority. When this takes place all three suffer: the marriage, the family, *and* the career. While there are occasions when it's essential to invest more time on one's career (starting a new business, studying for an advancement exam, etc.), I must caution for this occasion to be extremely short and we become hyper-cognizant of its effects on the marriage. Many a would-be Super Husband has come home to an empty, family-free house because he was so focused on his career he failed to comprehend the warning cries of his desperate spouse. Don't be that person! If you don't take the time to make central the spousal relationship, you will have no one left with which to share the spoils once your career is thriving.

I'd like to add one more consideration. When I was studying for my Ph.D., I felt as if I'd fail if my face weren't buried in a textbook 24/7. It made logical sense: the more time I spent the better the work I'd turn in or the better I'd retain. But after a while I found the opposite to be true. The more time devoted to my studies without a break, the more my brain became saturated and I became less productive. My mind would wander, my pace would slow, and my emotions would become frazzled. Over time, I realized that just because I was studying didn't mean I was learning. Eventually, I began to put everything down for a day (extremely difficult to do at first when it seemed I'd certainly fall behind on the two hundred pages of assigned daily reading) and I soon realized something amazing: when I allowed myself time to recharge and focus on my priorities—my spouse, my kids, and my sanity—I was able to do twice as much in half as much time. By maintaining proper focus I was able to return to my studies on Monday with renewed focus.

In what position is your spouse? Your children? Your career? Is there a lover? Only one can come first. Keep both and everyone loses. Attaining Super isn't effortless. Whether you choose to focus on your lover or your spouse, only one can grow in intimacy. Even if you have no lover, is your focus on your spouse, career, children, hobbies, or some other area of your life? Where are you setting your gaze? If your feelings for your spouse have disappeared, your gaze is likely not upon him/her. But know this—the feelings you once had *do* and *will* return. It's impossible for them not to. I am stating that not as some hopeful optimist but from educated certainty. How can I make such a bold statement? Simply this: because your love-producing actions worked once before. They will work again. Actions beget feelings.

I've alluded often to infidelity but you needn't have experienced that to fall short of a Super marriage. These principles are true even if you're in a content marriage but are not yet *extremely* happy. If you feel you've moved to a secondary priority in your spouse's heart or your spouse is secondary in *yours* then you might want to reexamine your relational priorities and reprioritize them. This may sound like a lot of work, and it is, but the payoff—an extremely happy marriage—is worth it.

Up to now we have learned what it takes to attain extreme happiness yet we've not answered: what is happiness anyway? I've learned how to make *my spouse* happy, but what about me? The good news is that focusing on our spouse's happiness will make *us* happy too—and we have science to prove it.

THE PURSUIT OF HAPPINESS

Of course we all want to be happy. Happiness is such a desired state of being that it was written into our founding documents. The United States' Declaration of Independence declares as a self-evident truth that we are all endowed with an unalienable right to pursue happiness. I'm good with that. I want to be just as happy as the next guy. The problem is that it underscores the truth by making happiness, like love, seem like something elusive, to be found and *pursued* until we are somehow lucky enough to catch it. But this is not the case.

Happiness is so desirable that science has gotten into the picture. So many researchers have sought to understand happiness that an entire new scientific field called *positive psychology* has emerged onto the academic landscape. For the most part, *positive psychology* is really just the study of happiness. While the field is expansive, for the sake of this book, I will break emerging research into practical language and apply it to our daily lives, specifically our marriages. So what is happiness?

In her book, *The How of Happiness* positive psychology researcher Sonja Lyubomirsky describes happiness as "the experience of joy, contentment, or positive well-being, combined with a sense that one's life is good, meaningful, and worthwhile (2007, pg. 32)." According to the Greater Good Science Center (GGSC) whose mission it is to help people apply groundbreaking scientific research of social and emotional well-being to their personal and professional lives and have been at the fore of a new scientific movement to explore "the science of a meaningful life" happiness, unelaborated, is the state of "subjective well-being," which is measured by people's self-reports of "how satisfied they feel with their own lives and how much positive and negative emotion they're experiencing." As this current research on love has shown, the scientists at GGSC assert that likewise happiness *can* and should be cultivated for its many benefits to both self and others. But, one of the most important benefits they assert relevant to this research on Super Couples is better relationships: "Happier people have more friends and are more likely to get married and have fulfilling marriages."

If we consider this final statement more closely it would seem to turn our understanding of the happy marriage on its head. Many believe, as I once did, that I'd be happier once I had a good marriage. While there is some truth in that, this statement points to the inverse: the happier I am *first* (remember, happiness is a choice) will result in a happier marriage as a by-product. Now I want to stop right here and say that I am not so Pollyanna-ish as to believe that all I have to do is choose to be happy and then all of my marital problems will go away. I am quite possibly one of the happiest people in the world. I love life and find joy in nearly everything I do. Had marital happiness really been nothing more than a matter of "choosing" then I would have been half of a Super Couple three decades ago. But I was not. That being said, many who tend to maintain more of a glass half-empty attitude could benefit greatly from a reassessment of their basic outlook on life in order to see a bit more that the glass is half full. Few wish to hang out with those toxic "woe is me" individuals who always seem to suck the joy out of every environment. So knowing one can cultivate his or her own happiness is a wonderful starting point along this journey to Super Couple and a basically happier you. I would strongly encourage you to do an honest self-assessment and focus first on improving your own personal levels of happiness before you move on to the more intricately involved marital happiness.

To get started at increasing your overall levels of personal happiness the researchers at GGSC have produced a list of some of the best ways to cultivate happiness. Three of the easiest are by exercising, resting, and practicing mindfulness. Regular physical activity they write "increases happiness and self-esteem, reduces anxiety and stress, and can even lift symptoms of depression." And many in our sleep-deprived nation are feeling the happiness-lowering consequences that researchers have linked to lower sleep. Jason Marsh, in his article, 'The Hows of Happiness" cites a 2010 study led by Nobel Prize-winning psychologist Daniel Kahneman and Angus Deaton of more than 900 women in which they found that "just one more hour of sleep each night might have a greater effect on happiness than a $60,000 raise." And lastly, though a bit less concrete in practice than exercising and sleeping more is the practice of mindfulness, which they define as "the moment-by-moment awareness of our thoughts, feelings and external circumstances." Researchers have found those who practice mindfulness strategies "not only have stronger immune systems but are more likely to be happy and enjoy greater life satisfaction." There are numerous inventories through which you can begin to gauge and assess your happiness and well-being and I would offer that a good place for you to start would be by going to http://greatergood. berkeley.edu/topic/happiness. You've got nothing to lose and will likely end up a bit happier you if you do.

While a happier overall personal attitude is an essential place to begin, having a happy marriage necessarily involves two people and is a bit more complex in its attainment. But before I enumerate the strategies essential to cultivating an extremely happy marriage I would first like to present a more in-depth understanding of the two types of happiness at the root of the aforementioned research: the short-termed and fleeting faux happiness that many of us spend our lives fruitlessly chasing— the same faux happiness our ancestors of every generation have unsuccessfully chased as well—and the true and lasting happiness that leads individuals and couples to Super.

HEDONIC HAPPINESS

Researchers have found that happiness can be broken into two basic types: hedonic and eudaimonic. Let's first consider the former. Hedonic happiness comes from the same root word as does hedonism and is certainly not new to modern society. Hedonism teaches that pleasure or happiness *is* the highest good. As such, hedonic happiness dictates that the formula for true happiness is based on having the sum difference between the greatest amount of pleasure and the least amount of pain in our everyday lives. In other words, hedonic happiness is seen as the "Good Life." If our jobs are good, we have a comfortable income, our families are healthy, we drive nice cars, etc., we will then attain happiness. If this were true it would follow that we would have little control of our own happiness. It would be, to some degree, out of our control. *Bummer. I have a low-paying job working with people I don't especially like, my parents or children are ailing, and my income is insufficient for my needs let alone my wants. I unfortunately am not able to be happy in this state of being.*

While this may sound over-exaggerated, it makes the point. Even if we have a great job with a good income, hedonic happiness would teach that if you are sick, or at an inappropriate weight or health status, have a sick parent or child to care for, or any other aspect of your life is not where you yet desire for it to be that your happiness—or lack thereof—is proportionate and partial. Hedonic happiness is *extrinsic,* which means it comes from outside your control. *"Now that sucks. I'm pursuing happiness and it continually eludes me. I guess I'm not one of the "lucky" ones."* Hedonic happiness would also presume then that Hollywood celebrities who certainly have attained all the hedonic pleasures in life (fame, fortune, and beauty) would be the happiest people in the world. Ha! Based on news stories and the number of Hollywood stars killing themselves and overdosing we can presume true happiness has eluded many of our celebrities as well—maybe more so than we commoners. And here's why.

In order to best describe hedonic happiness, let's consider something that makes you really happy. Let's just say that you are a huge fan of ice cream and you discover a new flavor that is absolutely amazing. I mean the flavor of this ice cream is one hundred times better than anything you've previously tasted—and it makes you happy. Well, hedonic happiness would dictate then that in order to stay happy you should eat that ice cream each and every day and you'll remain happy—or at least while it's melting over your taste buds. And to a degree it does make you happy. So you decide to have some of this ice cream every day. The problem is, however, that while the ice cream makes you happy, it makes you just a wee bit *less* happy the second time you eat it than it made you the first time you experienced the sweet and savory delicacy. So you need more of it. And it makes you happy—temporarily—but even less happy the third and the fourth times until eventually you find that it really doesn't make you happy at all. It's lost its glamour. It bores you. Worse yet, you may even start to *dislike* it for what it does to you—it results in your ultimate *lack* of happiness. Hedonic pleasure seeking is the reason there is such a big problem today with drugs, alcohol, pornography, gambling, overeating, or any other type of addiction. It is extremely pleasurable at first but over time it makes us less and less happy so we need more and more of it. The "high" we get from these extrinsic pleasures decreases with every exposure and we are left empty and our desires unsated— unhappy. Consider the man referenced previously who was addicted to the initial feelings of a sexual attraction such that he was a serial cheater. The love cocktail—those initial feelings of love—was his drug of choice and brought him temporary experiences of pleasure and happiness—hedonic happiness. The more he had the more he needed to satiate his appetite, and the more quickly the happiness would wear off. This is as it is with all extrinsic pleasures.

Hedonic happiness is not new to our society or to our generation. The concept of Ethical Hedonism goes back several millennia and is said to have been started by a student of Socrates, named Aristippus of Cyrene who held the idea that pleasure is the highest good (Encyclopedia of Religion and Ethics 6. p. 567). But the first recorded proof of the avocation of hedonism is found in the original Old Babylonian version of the Epic of Gilgamesh—perhaps the oldest written story on earth— written soon after the invention of writing, with the advice "Fill your belly. Day and night make merry. Let days be full of joy. Dance and make music day and night [...] these things alone are the concern of men." (Hedonism, Wikipedia)

Further, ancient Egyptian tomb drawings that sometimes contained hedonistic elements, called guests to submit to pleasure because they cannot be sure they will be rewarded for good with a blissful afterlife. The following is a song attributed to the reign of one of the Intef Kings before or after the Twelfth Dynasty, and the text was used in the Eighteenth and Nineteenth Dynasties:

Let thy desire flourish,
In order to let thy heart forget the beatifications for thee.
Follow thy desire, as long as thou shalt live.
Put myrrh upon thy head and clothing of fine linen upon thee,
Being anointed with genuine marvels of the gods' property.
Set an increase to thy good things;
Let not thy heart flag.
Follow thy desire and thy good.
Fulfill thy needs upon earth, after the command of thy heart,
Until there come for thee that day of mourning (Hedonism, Wikipedia).

Though the concept of hedonism predates the written word, our errant seeking of hedonic happiness has become a problem of epic proportions in our world today. Consider the flourishing industries that focus on our search for extrinsic happiness. The multibillion-dollar plastic surgery industry promises happiness through attainment of "perfect" faces and bodies. An entire genre of reality television shows has emerged that focuses on body makeovers, home makeovers, car makeovers–all material happiness. Are these persons happier with their newly made-over bodies, houses, and cars? If the understanding of hedonic happiness is applied to their lives they are likely to be *less* happy now that the initial euphoria of their improved selves has worn off.

Compare also, today's weddings with average weddings just thirty years ago when all that was needed for a successful wedding and happy couple was a venue, a preacher, and one's family and friends. Today, couples are encouraged to spend obscene amounts of money (often on credit) on their celebrations by renting castles and mansions, hiring performers such as acrobats and belly-dancers, and purchasing not one but two or more wedding dresses, and other sorts of wedding accoutrement. Anything less and a bride is made to feel her wedding is sub-standard compared to her contemporaries and thus her "happiness" unmet. This doesn't even include the modern rule that engagement rings must equal three months of the groom's income. Are you serious?

Unfortunately, many men are now bearing this new financial responsibility for his fiancé's happiness before they even walk down the aisle. After all, you wouldn't want her friends to think you are cheap or see her unhappy with a more humble-sized engagement ring now would you? Still, if all of these things created a lasting happiness then I say "Absolutely! Buy the ring the size of Texas and throw in a third wedding dress while you're at it." But alas, they do not. Like all hedonic happiness, the results from these extrinsic pleasures will, over time, wane and we will be left needing more: more stuff and more happiness.

In this new millennium we have bigger cars, bigger homes, and bigger toys (like motorcycles, boats, and snowmobiles) than did those only a century ago who longed to have even one of the above and worked many more hours just to have the little they did have. Many of us have housekeepers. We have luxuries like gym memberships, movie theaters visited with great frequency, amusement parks—places designed solely to provide pleasurable feelings and fun (unless, like my husband, you don't consider throwing up after a spin on the Teacups fun). We have huge wardrobes when our forefathers had only two or three changes of clothing. We have numerous pairs of shoes, specialized shoes for any activity such as running, weightlifting, tennis, walking. We have televisions in every room, personal computers and phones—one for every member of the household—so no one has to fight over them. You get the picture. Hedonic pleasures come with promises of great happiness and yet Americans are significantly less happy than they have ever been if gauged by the skyrocketing numbers of those being treated for depression and other stress-related disorders and problems—or worse— those attempting and succumbing to suicide. We have so much more material and hedonic pleasure than we once had and yet it is our *unhappiness* that is growing proportionately.

Research confirms these assertions. According to scholars, in order to find true happiness one must not focus on material wealth. In its page on happiness under "How to Cultivate Happiness?" The GGSC writes:

> After our basic needs are met, research suggests, more money doesn't bring us more happiness—in fact, a study by Kahneman found that Americans' happiness rose with

their income only until they'd made roughly $75,000; after that, their happiness plateaued. And research by Richard Easterlin has found that in the long run, countries don't become happier as they become wealthier. Perhaps that's why, in general, people who prioritize material things over other values are much less happy, and comparing ourselves with people who have more is a particular source of unhappiness. It also suggests why more egalitarian countries consistently rank among the happiest in the world ("Happiness," 2013).

So, in short, "stuff" does not make us happy. But don't be discouraged for true happiness is not as elusive as the above paragraphs may cause you to believe. As stated earlier, researchers have begun to uncover the causes of true and lasting happiness. In truth, the formula is not new, only the science illuminating it. Since so much validity is placed in the Scientific Method these days it will be comforting for you to have the obvious confirmed and explained—especially as it applies to true relational and marital happiness.

EUDAIMONIC HAPPINESS

When we focus on the self-centric and fleeting material happiness of hedonism, happiness eludes us. But when we focus on more other-centric thoughts and practices, true happiness becomes attainable. The name for this type of happiness is eudaimonic.

Before I explain eudaimonia, let me first tell you several ways it can be cultivated. I believe you will then immediately begin to understand what leads to true and lasting happiness in our lives and marriages. According to Lyubomirsky and other researchers, some of the best ways to cultivate happiness is by:

- Giving thanks: Research by Michael McCullough, Robert Emmons, Lyubomirsky, and others has revealed the power of simply counting our blessings on a regular basis. People who keep "gratitude journals" feel more optimism and greater satisfaction with their lives. And research shows that writing a "gratitude letter" to someone you've never properly thanked brings a major boost of happiness.

- Practicing kindness: Research by Elizabeth Dunn and her colleagues finds that people report greater happiness when they spend money on others than when they spend it on themselves, even though they initially think the opposite would be true. Similarly, neuroscience research shows that when we do nice things for others, our brains light up in areas associated with pleasure and reward.

- Giving up grudges: Groundbreaking studies by Everett Worthington, Michael McCullough, and their colleagues show that when we forgive those who have wronged us, we feel better about ourselves, experience more positive emotions, and feel closer to others.

The final key finding reported by the scholars at GGSC regarding cultivating true happiness is perhaps the most relative to this research: building relationships. They write that, "Perhaps the dominant finding from happiness research is that social connections are key to happiness. Studies show that close relationships, including romantic relationships, are especially important, suggesting we should make time for those closest to us—people in whom we can confide and who'll support us when we're down."

The word "eudaimonia" comes from the Greek words that together mean "good spirit" or "well-being" and it seems telling that this type of happiness pronounced: YOU-DUH-MONIC begins by putting "You" (and not me) first. The concept of eudaimonia is central in Aristotelian Ethics as well as the Greek word areté which is usually translated into English as the words "virtue" or "excellence." Aristotle describes eudaimonia as "the highest human good" and "human flourishing." Unlike its brother hedonism, which is short-termed, fleeting, and decreases in pleasure over time, eudaimonic happiness produces long-term results and actually *increases* the more of it one has or I should say the more of it one *practices*. While hedonic happiness is based on extrinsic reward, the rewards gained from eudaimonic happiness are intrinsic.

So what does this mean? Eudaimonia can be better explained as the "pay-it-forward" happiness. Crazy isn't it? Research has found that people are most happy when they focus on *giving* rather than *receiving,* when they focus more on the *other* than the *self.* I am sure you are having a "no-duh" moment right now as did I when I first learned of this but it was still nonetheless amazing to me to see that science confirmed what my mother had always taught me: put others before yourself and it will always warm your heart—you will be happy. Amazing.

Have you ever volunteered in a soup kitchen, or worked with the homeless, or with any other disadvantaged population? Have you ever given time or money to someone else who, though you definitely needed it, needed it more? Have you ever placed money into the palm of a hungry man or mowed the lawn of an elderly neighbor? Have you ever paid for the meal of the person behind you in the drive through because the person ahead of you paid for yours? I have and it felt great to hear "Ma'am, your order has been paid for. Would you like to pass on the favor?" It felt even better driving off knowing I'd just done the same. Eudaimonia. Each time you selflessly gave of yourself to one of these others you were experiencing the intrinsic rewards of eudaimonic happiness.

My family used to attend a church that collected food and gifts for the poorest of the poor in our city and delivered those gifts to each family a few days prior to the Christmas holiday. I'm sure your church, synagogue, or workplace has likely done something similar. While most collection sites collect and wrap the gifts and food once purchased by the generous donors, not all programs allow (for privacy reasons) for the delivery directly to specific houses by the churchgoers. We were lucky (though we hadn't yet realized it) that we were able to do so. At this particular church we picked a name off the Angel tree that had the age and gender of a child or adult as well as his or her shoe and clothing sizes and purchased a gift or two for that person. Because the gifts were going to those who often couldn't afford to eat, no requests for toys or other non-essentials were listed on the Angel tag though that didn't always stop one from adding a small toy or non-essential item.

On one particular Christmas week my family was given grocery bags filled with a turkey or ham, enough groceries for a complete, yet humble, Christmas dinner for a family of seven and fourteen individually wrapped gifts—two per person—each marked with the tags from the Angel tree. We were sent to the poorest (and dare I say the most dangerous) part of our city with nothing more than the address of the recipients. My husband, myself, and both of our daughters were together on this brisk, dark winter day and I must admit, we were in a hurry to do what it was we needed to do and quickly leave for whatever event we had next on our schedule for that day, you know, something extremely important like dinner with friends or maybe a date with our television and a Green Bay Packers game...or more Christmas shopping. Imperative stuff. I could see my daughters' bored expressions through the rearview mirror as we headed to our destination—looks that said, "Hurry up and get this over with. Why did you have to take us anyway? You could have done this without us." My daughters were seven and ten at the time.

As we pulled up to the ill-repaired building on a city block where every other home was equally as worn and dilapidated, I got out of the car and slowly walked up the broken steps to the front entrance. I knocked on the door and it was partially and apprehensively opened by a sweet and well-mannered twelve-year-old boy who managed a gentle "Hi." When I asked if his mom was home he said she was in the restroom—obviously a well-practiced response from a child who'd likely been left alone frequently while his mother was probably at work earning whatever she could to feed her family. Based on the ages and genders on the Angel tags we knew there was no adult male in this household.

After introducing myself I let him know that my family and I were there to bring them a few things for Christmas and asked if it would be okay for us to bring them up to the front door and place them on the porch?

"I guess so."

With that he opened the door widely exposing a house with only a few pieces of furniture: a couch, an end table and a lampstand. There were no rugs, only sheets for curtains, only handmade children's artwork on the walls, a small television propped on the seat of a wooden chair and, most notably, a very small "Charlie Brown" Christmas tree in the corner of the room with no tree skirt and no presents underneath—not even one. On it was a strand or two of lights and a smattering of handmade, paper ornaments. My heart was immediately saddened to know that people had to live with so little while my children had never gone a day without a meal or material pleasures. I quickly glanced down the hallway and noticed that the scarcity of "stuff" extended far beyond what I saw in front of me.

At my signal, my husband then exited the car with the two bags of groceries in each arm and handed them to the young boy—his face revealing a look of bewilderment at the unexpected gift. "These are for your Christmas dinner" he quietly told the boy and turned to retrieve the gifts from the trunk. The young boy and I followed him. My daughters now exited the car seemingly gaining a greater awareness of our mission and turned to meet us at the now open trunk. My husband placed a gift in Gabrielle's hands—my seven-year-old—a couple more gifts into the arms of my ten-year-old Jessica, and two more into the arms of this young boy. With gifts in mine and my husband's arms as well, we followed him up to his front door where he took the time to place each gift gently under the tree, his look of astonishment growing ever more evident. As we handed them to him we read the tags "This one is for a three-year-old girl."

"Oh that's my baby sister Bella!"

"And this one says a seven-year-old boy."

"That's Sam's! That must be Sam's! Wow that looks pretty big!"

We continued this gift-handling and identification process until we got to the very last presents. And I promise you not for the sake of exaggerating a story for this book but rather, as if divinely planned the very last two gifts tied together with ribbon said "twelve-year-old boy." As this final gift was handed to this sweet and gentle boy, he looked up and said "For *me?* There's one for *me* too?" It seemed as if in his tender heart that though he saw gifts for each of his family members, including his mother, something deep down prevented him from assuming there'd be one for him as well. (Possibly a lifetime of barren Christmases where few, if any, gifts were ever found under the tree Christmas morning had conditioned him to expect nothing.) I will never forget how he clutched this shirt-box sized gift to his chest and just stood there for what seemed like five minutes (but was probably more like five seconds). Immediately thereafter the largest smile ever seen on a twelve-year-old stretched across his beautiful face—the kind of happy smile that stays on your face the entire day of your wedding or after you've just delivered your newborn baby.

We wished him a merry Christmas and from our respective seats in our car we watched him until he entered his house reminding him not to forget to lock the door behind him. As my husband pulled away our car remained blessedly silent for none of us wanted to speak and lose the spirit of what we had just experienced—each of us obviously touched by the emotionally powerful interchange we had just been a part of. Finally, after about five minutes I heard the voice of my seven-year-old, "Can we do that again next year?" I knew exactly what she meant and yes, we absolutely would do that again next year.

What my daughter articulated and we all felt that day was the intrinsic by-product of eudaimonic happiness—the highest human good—whereupon we put someone else's needs before our own and our souls began to flourish. We were happy—truly happy. Here it is more than two decades later and that short fifteen-minute interchange is still seared in my mind's eye as if it had just occurred last Christmas. Unlike the long since forgotten material gifts I received that year that appealed to my hedonistic nature, the happiness produced by that eudaimonic experience increases my happiness each subsequent time I think about it. Good stuff, hey?

Have you ever seen the television series *Secret Millionaire?* In each episode a millionaire goes undercover into disadvantaged communities to work alongside poor but extremely compassionate and appreciative individuals or charities whose only goals are to do all they can for a forgotten or neglected part of their community. Little do they know the new "volunteers" working alongside them and getting to know them are millionaires who will reveal their true identities at the end of their week. When this "reveal" takes place the millionaires also present to these individuals and charities large gifts of cash to cover educational costs, medical expenses, pay off mortgages and cars, or to be used as seed money to build the infrastructure the financially-strapped individuals envisioned but could never before afford.

Likewise, in *Undercover Boss,* a corporate CEO disguises him or herself and works alongside the company's frontline staff to observe practices that work exceptionally well or are bordering on failure with the intent of using the newfound knowledge to improve the overall company from the top levels down. However, just as in *The Secret Millionaire* the residual relationships that are forged in this process inspire the executives to go beyond that which can certainly help the company improve its bottom line—the *receiving* of new knowledge and better practices—to the *giving* of their own funds to those individuals alongside whom they worked. The executives will help their employees by giving them deserved promotions, increased pay, better equipment to work with and numerous improvements to their work lives. However, so touched are most of these executives by one or more of the individual staff members that they will give to them gifts that will benefit them and their families personally as did the secret millionaires.

The unexpected beauty of these shows is seen not through the tear-stained faces of the individuals who have just received these life-altering gifts but rather in the faces and the hearts of those who had *given* them. One secret millionaire once said that he was so overwhelmed by the emotional impact this event had on his life that he was now going to make a regular habit of giving back. I am certain he was not alone.

What each of these millionaires experienced was eudaimonic happiness—and it was not only intoxicating but addictive. The intrinsic value of this event had lasting effects on them and their lives so much so that they wanted to give more of themselves. Herein lays the essence of eudaimonia. Unlike the very sel*fish* nature of hedonic happiness—the more **I** have the more **I** need—the sel*fless* nature of eudaimonic happiness is other-centric: the more I *give* the more I want *to continue giving* and my spirit flourishes. These millionaires and undercover bosses experienced the highest human good by giving to others above themselves...and they were happy...*happier* than if they'd have kept their gifts to themselves.

So what does all this mean for the Super Couple?

When applying these positive psychology findings to marital happiness something amazingly powerful becomes illuminated:

by seeking to meet first the needs of my spouse—focusing on the happiness of the other over the self—not only is my spouse happier but *I* am actually happier in my marriage.

I loved doing these interviews. Going into each new home and observing each different Super Couple always brought about so much peace and contentment for me as I eventually came to understand that Super Couples were skilled practitioners of eudaimonia within their marriages. I never wanted to leave those homes. Super Couples made serving one another an art form.

For far too many years of my marriage my focus was on what Danny was *not* doing for me or my unmet needs. *"Why don't you talk with me more? Why can't you buy me flowers? When are we going to watch my TV shows?"* Of course they weren't usually this simplistic. They were often more abstract or unarticulated needs such as *"Why won't you speak up more? Why won't you defend my honor in public? Why do you always tell everyone all I do is complain?" "Why can't you be more like me?"* While most of these may seem somewhat noble in terms of wanting to improve the marital relationship, their underlying implications were that my spouse should be the one to change to please me (which actually, he should—we all should) but *my* focus was still on *me* and *my* happiness while his focus was on him and his happiness. In essence, I was still focusing more on what would make *me* happier in the marriage with much less concern for what would make Dan happier. Dan was often doing the same. *"Why do you talk so much? I don't want to eat dinner at the table. I've had a long day. Why can't you just leave me alone for a while? I don't feel like going to that event with you. Why can't you just sit here and watch television with me?"*

Now let's be clear. Dan and I both believed we loved each other. I mean, we told each other we loved each other daily. And I am certain we both wanted to be happy—and happily married. However, if one simply focuses on the underlying nature of our statements to the other a pattern would be noticed. Both Dan and I—like most every other *unsuper* couple—were focusing on the happiness of the self over happiness of the other. I definitely wanted Dan to be happy but my focus was on my own happiness first. The same held true for him. Though these statements may not immediately point to hedonistic happiness, they most certainly were, because their focus was on meeting the needs of the self above the other—taking. Remember, hedonic happiness is extrinsic and based on external factors that I have little to no control of. And I had no control over Dan nor he over me. Though I wasn't basing my happiness on wealth or material possessions; I was still focusing on me.

Super Couples turn this thinking on its head.

As I've said before, the same series of questions was asked in every Super Couple interview. Three questions in particular helped me to better understand this practice of eudaimonia within these marriages. Those questions were:

1. What makes you a Super Couple, yours a Super marriage?
2. What do you have that other couples don't?
3. What, to you, are the main ingredients in "Super Couple" marriages?

It only took me about five interviews to notice a pattern emerge and that the responses to these were nearly the same every time. For Super Husbands, the responses to each of these questions pointed *always* to their wives: we are Super because *she* is Super. Said Larry, "There was a time when my mother lived with us and *my wife* cared for her even though she was bi-polar and always trying to destroy our relationship." Said Rob, "Maggie would never even think about letting us pay a penny of interest. She is exceptional at taking care of our budget and family." For Super Wives it was equally reciprocal. Jenny claimed, "This man! Let me tell you about this amazing man..." Lisa, "I adore my husband. He is definitely the reason." And so on.

Interview after interview husbands pointed to wives and wives pointed to husbands as the reason for their Superness. This was captured not in singular phrases but in the overall tone of the interviews. There was a carefulness of speech, a complimentary dialogue and naturalness where each spouse thoughtfully put the other spouse first. And this wasn't contrived. This is just what I observed. But their selfless focus on their spouse wasn't just apparent in their words, it was apparent in their deeds as well. Super Couples *served* one another regularly.

One Super Wife talked about how she would get up and iron her husband's clothes at 5:00 every morning because he liked to have newly pressed clothing every day and then she'd go back to sleep as soon as he left. I asked why she didn't just iron his clothes the night before so she could remain asleep and she responded "Because *he* liked putting on the newly ironed clothes while they were warm." I asked why he didn't do them himself— did he *expect* her to do the ironing—to which she responded "Absolutely not. He had been doing his own ironing for years. I like ironing for him because it gives us time together every morning before he leaves and, after all, he likes it. It makes him happy. Why would I not want to make him happy?" I guess she told me.

I hear similar selfless responses when we talk about sex as well. While sex is important to each of these couples to varying degrees and they all agree the richness of their sex lives has been greatly enhanced by their time together and years of growing in love for one another, their frequency of sex has changed over the years (some more often, some less often). But one thing remained apparent: their sexual relationships are also enhanced by the selflessness of one or both spouses in these couples.

Remember that at the onset of my research (and for many decades before) I held the idealized assumption that these Super Couples continued to have the mad, passionate, four times a day love-making experiences that they did in their youth—that we all did in our youth—when our love cocktails were still fully active. Of course this notion was and continues to be fueled by the media portrayals we are exposed to—but these are Super Couples, the best of the best, surely *they* experienced something different than the rest of us. But alas, while their love cocktail hormones eventually leveled off like the rest of the population, one thing these couples continued to practice even in their love-making was the same selflessness they practiced in the other areas of their marriage as well.

A few years ago I was discussing this topic with one Super Wife. I asked her if she enjoyed having sex as much and as often as did her husband. She responded that sex wasn't important to her at all—that she could go significantly longer without it than could her husband. However, this Super Wife also pointed out that she couldn't remember the last time she'd refused her husband when he pursued her. Asking her why not she responded, "Well, I know how much it means to him. It makes him happy. And if all I have to do is sacrifice a little time in my schedule to please him, why would I not? And besides, whenever I need to go shopping or spend money on something that I want he lets me—because it makes *me* happy."

Remember when we discussed in our section on dating how Duane would come home and spend the first hour of his time in devoted conversation with his wife? I know Duane to be a solid introvert: he'd rather think and listen than speak. He had no innate "desire" to come home and talk—especially after having done so all day in his position as a sales rep in a high-performing field. Additionally, Gina and Duane also made a guest "appearance" on my radio show a couple of times. Duane said he'd rather have a tooth pulled without anesthesia than to be on the air discussing his private marriage with several thousand strangers throughout the nation. I was doing a series on Super Couples and convinced them to come on and grace my listeners with their secret to a happy marriage as they had done with me in our interview. So I asked him why he was willing to do so. His response of course was because it made Gina happy. Duane, like all of my Super Spouses in the examples above as well as the many examples not on these pages, submitted his own needs to second position behind those of his wife. Duane knew innately, or had come to learn over time, that when Gina was happy that he, too, was happy. And he liked it.

Super Couples are expert practitioners of the pay-it-forward aspect of eudaimonic happiness, and as the number of selfless acts increases throughout their years of marriage, their happiness increases proportionately. When this pattern of reciprocal selflessness becomes habitual these marriages flourish.

Putting this principle on paper seems so easy. The idea that almost forty percent of couples divorce points to the fact that they are clearly not happy. Further, because they are unhappy (and thus not practicing eudaimonia) it illustrates, however, that being selfless is much easier said than done. But why? Why would I not want to make my spouse happy? Why would I not want to be happy? The simple answer? Because most of us are unaware of the principles of eudaimonia in our lives and in our marriages or we'd be practicing them. The not so simple answer? Because it's risky. If I focus all my energy on meeting *your* needs how can I be sure that you will be focusing your energy on meeting mine? Well, to be honest, you can't be sure.

Consider the wife born and raised in sunny Florida, who hates the cold and suffers from seasonal depression. To support her husband's career she told him she'd move wherever he decided to go if it would help him get promoted. On a particular day her husband came home and informed her that he had been offered equal positions in both Arizona and Alaska, states where neither had any family or connections. After expressing her preference for Arizona for the reasons mentioned above she trusted he'd consider her needs and choose Arizona. One week later she found out he'd taken the position in Alaska because it provided some of the best fishing in America and he was an avid fisherman. In this example, the wife put her husband's needs before her own by telling him she'd support his career by moving wherever that career took them—even though it meant quitting her own job and starting anew elsewhere. She trusted he'd seek to meet her needs as well. He did not. He, too, put his needs for fishing above her needs for a warmer climate. This is selfish and anything but eudaimonic. Should this pattern persist, this couple is destined for problems.

It was difficult for me in those unhappy years to focus on my husband's needs because I was hurting and empty. The thought of surrendering my needs and focusing on Dan's was risky for if I focused on his needs alone I had no assurance he'd be focused on meeting mine.

For the most part, your spouse is a good person and sincerely wants you to be happy. This is true for most, or you wouldn't have married them in the first place. However, there are three prime reasons why our spouses generally neglect to meet our needs. First, we often assume we have the same needs, which we usually do not. Second, should our spouses *realize* we don't have the same needs they often don't know what those differing needs are, and third, once they can *identify* those needs they have little idea how to meet them. Let's consider this first reason—assuming our needs are the same.

I love parties—big parties with lots of people, noise, food, and fun. Oh, and I love surprise parties even more. As you know by now I am an off-the-charts-extrovert so this should not surprise you at all. As such, when my strongly introverted husband was about to turn thirty I threw him the biggest, loudest, surprise party ever to take place on the east coast. While Dan was likely happy that I had thought about him, and while he enjoyed himself the entire day of celebration, Dan would have preferred to usher in his thirties quietly: at home with no more than his daughters and me and an ice cream cake with candles. Though I'm not sure I knew that at the time, I'm pretty certain I'd have thrown him the big party anyway because who doesn't like a great big surprise party?

So two years later on the eve of my thirtieth birthday I was absolutely hurt when I found out that not only did my husband have nothing planned for my birthday, but that I had to make my own arrangements to spend the day with a few of my girlfriends. We went out to dinner. While I loved that my sweet friends made time to spend that momentous birthday with me, I was so disappointed in my husband's perceived "lack of consideration" that I told him so—every birthday for the next decade.

Have you ever heard the phrase "Do unto others as you would have them do unto you"? Most have. In the above example Dan and I were both being stellar practitioners of that mantra. In planning for Dan the surprise party of the century I was treating him exactly as I would have wanted to be treated. And in leaving me to plan my own small dinner party Dan did the same. So here's the problem. While the phrase, at its core, is quite altruistic, it would be better expressed "Do unto others as *they* would have you do unto *them*." Though Dan and I loved each other, we failed to meet each other's needs because we simply assumed their needs were the same as ours. First mistake.

The second is similar. Even should we know that our spouse's needs are different from our own, there still usually exists an inability to identify what your spouse's needs actually are. The primary reason is that we, ourselves, are often unable to identify our needs either. When I left my husband in 1987 I knew that I was unhappy. But if you'd have asked me to articulate why, I could not have succinctly done so. I likely would have listed a few examples such as "I didn't like it when you said ABC" or "I hate it when you shut me out during an argument" but even that's a stretch. Sometimes all we can identify is how we *felt* during particular fights but few of us can easily identify the unmet need causing the hurt, pain or frustration. We need time and contemplation to do so. Looking back thirty years through the wiser lens of one whose education and experiences have garnered for her a greater self-awareness, I am now able to say that back in 1987 I had an unmet need for intimate communication with my spouse. Our communication was infrequent at best and when we did converse it was unproductive and filled with hurtful and sarcastic remarks. Dan was a stuffer and I was an escalator. I would scream and he would shut down. It was quite a sight to behold (that's sarcasm in case you were wondering). But at 22 and 24 respectively our ignorance of our own needs was to be expected. Had I been able to say "Dan, I have a great need for improved communication and it's being unmet," I am certain Dan and I could have begun to find ways to address the issue and, with outside help, begin to meet the need.

Are you able to articulate all of your marital and emotional needs? Probably not. Even so, are you able to articulate to your spouse how to best meet your unmet needs? Also unlikely. It would follow then that your spouse is equally as unlikely to know how to meet those needs. But let's assume you can, in fact, articulate your unmet needs. Are you able to articulate the meaningful ways in which you desire to have those needs met? While you may be answering affirmatively today, would you have been able to do so five years ago? I used to struggle with Dan's lack of emotional expression. For years I wasn't even able to identify that lack. Once I was able to recognize that need, I did a poor job of getting Dan to understand what "emotional expression" meant. He thought it meant I wanted him to be a girl—a tenderhearted crybaby like me who emoted constantly, which wasn't the case. I liked having a strong and confident husband. It took me many years to communicate to Dan that emotional expression meant the ability to share *any* emotion with me—soft or hard emotions. I wanted him to be able to say things like "I don't want to go to your friend's house because I feel *annoyed* every time she starts talking about her colleagues." Did you know what I meant when I said emotional expression?

If so, then great. You're a step ahead. If not, then point made. How can you fix that which you don't clearly understand?

If you find yourself in these examples I suggest you become proactive and seek ways to improve skills in these areas. Begin by reading marriage or relationship books. Each new author seemed to be able to articulate for me something I was unable to recognize myself. Attend marriage seminars or conflict management classes. And always consider proactively seeking counseling to have that objective perspective by one trained to see what may not be obvious to us.

So this explains this threefold problem of unmet needs in our marital relationships that lead to lack of happiness. We must realize we have differing needs, be able to identify them and know how to remedy them. Only then can we begin to expect our spouse to meet them. Unless young spouses have been educated (directly or through modeling) in how to be happy and make their spouses happy, many will fall into this self-focused pattern of hedonistic happiness early on in their marriages. Over time, the pattern of "you're not meeting my needs so I'm not going to meet yours" gets established and perpetuated. "You don't meet my communication needs so I'm not meeting your sexual needs, etc." It becomes a negative cycle and someone needs to break it. That requires the aforementioned risk so few are willing to take.

At the end of my seminars I am often asked this very question by those who have found themselves in this same negative cycle. "Who should go first?" My answer is always the same: "*You* should." While this initially disheartens Super Spouse wannabes, I remind them that at its core, taking the first step in meeting their spouse's needs is the first step in attaining eudaimonic happiness. *If you want to be happier in your marriage then surrender all of your needs to those of your spouse. Put theirs in priority position—consistently.*

I did a radio show today on the topic of sacrifice and suffering in which my guest and I discussed these very principles. Ray's wife loves watching the show *The Bachelor*. Ray can't stand it. "However," Ray said, "every Monday night my wife and I sit together on the couch and watch *The Bachelor*. Well," he continues, "she watches it and I sit next to her reading. But at least we're together." But often times Ray says he looks over and sees just how happy his wife is and even without words her body language says to him "Thank you, Ray. This really means a lot to me." And he says it's all worth it. In this example, Ray sacrificed his own needs to meet Tina's needs and ultimately *his* happiness increases as well. Though some assume he had to "suffer" by not doing what *he* wanted, he was experiencing, rather, the pay-it-forward benefits of putting another before himself. Over time, if Ray continued to meet Tina's needs and she didn't reciprocate or appreciate his efforts, their relationship would become lopsided and Ray would lose the energy to please Tina. But in most cases this does not happen. Eudaimonia is addictive and thus it often becomes reciprocated. Since Tina is no longer expending as much energy meeting her own needs, she has more energy to focus on meeting Ray's needs. She may not always surrender the remote control to his favorite TV show but she may reciprocate it in other ways such as sharing his favorite activity with him after work. Though the activity itself may bring her no pleasure, knowing that it makes Ray happy does. And so the cycle begins.

For those in unhappy marriages the good news is that the cycle can also be reversed, as it was in my own marriage. As I said earlier, watching and listening to my Super Couples interact during interviews unknowingly helped me bring great changes in my interactions with Dan. I can't say it was totally subconscious because I intentionally began to practice some of what I was learning. Instead of asking Dan to do something for me I found myself doing something for him instead. I'd bring him his plate or let him have control of the television (unless deer hunting was on. I drew the line at deer hunting). Watching these couples interact made me argue less and accept Dan's opinion more—even when I disagreed—if it was too insignificant to argue about. I would go for walks with him more often (I preferred to run) because it made him happy. In essence, these interviews brought for me a bit of private shame once I recognized my own previously unnoticed selfishness. How could I have been so blind to my own self-focused attitude? Why was this not obvious before? Fortunately, things changed little by little. Rather than leaning towards an "all about me" attitude I considered more often "What would Dan want?" and it started to work.

I'm not sure if Dan consciously noticed my changed demeanor from hedonic to eudaimonic, but a beautiful thing began to happen nonetheless: Dan started to reciprocate my kindnesses. I didn't notice huge changes at first but subtle ones. He'd occasionally make the bed without being asked because he knew it made me happy. He'd go to chick flicks without arguing about how much he hated them...because I liked them. The negative cycle of "Why can't you do ABC for me?" and "Well, you didn't do XYZ for me!" was soon halted and then slowly began to spin in the opposite direction: the more Dan focused on my needs the happier I was and thus the happier he was. Moreover, I now wanted to focus on his needs more often because of the thoughtfulness he showed me. Additionally, the more I focused on his needs the happier I was. Wow! I began to see that Super wasn't impossible for us after all and my positive attitude toward my marriage began to materialize for the very first time in decades. I don't know if I can sufficiently communicate the deep emotional happiness this newfound awareness brought my soul. After decades of believing I'd never be happy with this man and would be relegated to a marriage of toleration, my heart began to burst. And I was humbled. "Thank you Jesus! We really could one day attain Super if we tried hard enough or, should I say, if we *loved* frequently enough.

Now that I've encouraged you that an extremely happy marriage is within *your* reach as well, I must add a bit of cautionary advice. While you now realize that serving your spouse and making his or her happiness your greatest priority will make *you* happier, it is imperative to keep in mind that serving your spouse in the same ways can, over time, become mundane, expected and thus lose its power to produce the same eudaimonic results.

As mentioned earlier, I love it when Dan surprises me with flowers. I love getting flowers and even leave an empty vase on the table on occasion as a hint that I sure would love to be surprised with another bouquet. He doesn't always catch the hint. But when he does it makes me very happy—not because I received flowers but because he loved me enough to think to purchase them. They become an outward sign of his desire to please me. Since this is less frequent an occurrence than I would like, the receiving of flowers has yet to lose its glamour with me. However, let's imagine that Dan has brought me flowers each and every week for the past thirty years. Would I still be happy to receive them? Possibly. But because I am human I, like everyone else, would begin to expect these flowers and my excitement at receiving them would diminish. My appreciation for Dan's efforts would be diminished. Further, it is equally likely the purchasing of flowers would become for Dan more of a habit than a "thought" and he, too, would no longer experience eudaimonic happiness. In this sense, the purchasing and receiving of flowers will now have crossed back into the realm of hedonic happiness—the more I have the more I need. Routine breeds hedonic happiness.

What needs to happen now to make you happy is to receive something different or receive nothing at all (for a time) and for your spouse to find another way to please you or show that you are still the center of his world. So here is the real trick to maintaining eudaimonic happiness: you must exhibit a consistent and thoughtful focus on finding new ways to please your spouse daily—make striving to please them a conscious and habitual occurrence.

So to bring this chapter full circle let me reiterate that to truly please your spouse and create for yourselves an extremely happy marriage your task is to behave in the last fifty or sixty years of your marriage in the same ways toward your spouse that you behaved in the first years when you were still trying to win his/her heart—in ways that made your spouse the center of your attentions. In the first years of your relationship your love grew because there were myriad ways you sought to please your young love interest. Those efforts not only brought your lover pleasure but you as well and those efforts reprioritized in your relationship, will renew your happiness and love. Remember, happiness and love are self-perpetuating phenomena.

Part IV:

WHAT I SAW:
THE SUPER COUPLE
FORMULA

As I set out on this academic journey of love I had no idea I'd be detailing the formula to Superness because, back then, I wasn't yet aware a formula existed. What a blessed outcome! In my striving for mere marital happiness I was able to discover the secret to *extreme* marital happiness instead. But I do believe marital Superness was never meant to be a secret. It was right before our eyes through the daily interactions of those many couples who made extreme marital happiness their lifetime priority. However, though visible, the formula was not obvious. No one had ever clearly delineated the formula. As such, I now present the Super Couple formula in order that you, too, are able to put them into practice in your own marriage. In contemplating how to do this, I realized that Super marriages were nothing short of SACRED. They require Selflessness, Attentiveness, Communication, Respect, Encouragement, and Deliberateness. Allow me now to fully develop those constructs to create for you a practical way of applying them to your own soon-to-be Super relationships.

SC PRINCIPLE #1: SELFLESSNESS
LOVE DOES NOT SEEK ITS OWN INTERESTS...

Just last weekend I interviewed Pete and Jenny. As in every interview I asked them "When did you *know* he/she was 'the one'?" Pete was describing the time he was deployed for a week and so he asked his "friend" Jenny if she wouldn't mind feeding his fish while he was away. Jenny lived about a half hour from his apartment and as a nineteen-year-old college student engrossed in academic responsibilities of her own, doing so was really more of a responsibility than simply pouring dehydrated fish flakes on a school of starving guppies. Of course, Jenny agreed—not because she had any feelings for Pete but more so because he was a military service member and Jenny had deep respect for the military. While at Pete's apartment she not only fed his fish but also cleaned his bedroom. She jokingly said it was not to impress Pete but for the "love of humanity"—since no one should ever have to be exposed to those conditions let alone *live* in them." In seriousness, she said it was the least she could do. That's all. When Pete came home and noticed what Jenny had done above and beyond his request he said "he knew" right then that Jenny would be more than a friend. When asked if it was because she cleaned his room he responded "No. It wasn't that she cleaned my room but rather that she *wanted* to do so."

If I were made to choose only one word to sum up Super marriages it would be selfless. For a word defined as "having little or no concern for oneself" it becomes obvious why selflessness is in such short supply in today's "all about me" society. Yet Super Couples seem to do this effortlessly. Selflessness is the cornerstone of Super marriages. All else is secondary. This was witnessed in interview after interview in both word and deed. Super Husbands were constantly putting their wives before themselves in all things as were Super Wives their husbands. We've witnessed numerous examples of this throughout the preceding chapters from Ray's watching *The Bachelor* because his wife liked it so much, to Duane's nightly conversations with Gina and their appearances on my radio show because it made Gina happy, to Paula's ironing of Larry's clothes at 5:30 AM because he liked it that way. But the selflessness ran deeper than simply the physical actions discussed. It was seen in the ways the questions were answered—ways that the couples themselves were not even cognizant of. Whenever asked to articulate a marital strength each immediately pointed to the other. Asked to articulate a difficulty each pointed to the self.

Cynical readers may question the respondents' motives or sincerity but it was not contrived. There was no guile. No ego-based attempt to answer the "right way" for the sake of the interviewer. Super Couples exposed a pattern of marital need-meeting wherein each sought to surrender his own needs to meet the needs of the other. In doing so, marital needs were constantly being met but by one's spouse. What's more it seemed each counted it a privilege to do so as if being able to serve their spouse was the greatest gift they could give the other. And it was.

When asked "What makes you a Super Couple and yours a Super marriage?" Lisa responded, "*I think if we compare what we have to what our friends and other people have...We don't argue. We don't fight. We respect one another. We put each other first.*

Jack added, "*I think that's the key there. We put each other first. A lot of people look at it as, "what's in it for me?" and when you get to that place, the other partner reciprocates. If you are constantly thinking about the other person and how to help them, it makes the marriage much better. A lot of people have selfish reasons for marriage. Ultimately you're in a marriage because you want a good thing for you. I think a lot of people focus on their own happiness. It's the way a lot of people think nowadays.*"

"What do you have that other couples don't?" I asked Larry and Paula.

"*I think they're selfish,*" responded Paula. Larry added, "*That may be the one quality that dooms a whole lot of marriages. Selfishness from both parts, and if you're going to be married there's no room for selfishness. There's just no room in marriages for selfishness. If selfishness creeps in, then you've already got some trouble. How do you fix that?*"

Though several couples readily acknowledged the insidiousness of selfishness within a marriage others exemplified it through their actions during the interview. I struggle to choose the words that capture the love and selflessness witnessed between each couple. I was humbled as it magnified the selfishness I had inflicted upon my own marriage to its detriment.

I'm sorry.

I'm sorry because I now know what a poor example of a spouse I was to my children, my colleagues, my church family, and all others who were forced to witness my own selfish expectations and complaints. I had a responsibility to model this institution in a way that edified the larger community and I failed. The good news though is that is no longer. Knowledge is power and while I cannot undo any past damage I'd caused by my marital selfishness, I could absolutely create a new pattern. And that's exactly what I did. I began a quest to serve my spouse at every opportunity above myself. Sometimes it was easy, much of the time it was not. But it got easier over time. Serving my husband began to please me and made me feel more like a Super Wife. However, when Dan or any husband seeks to please his wife not only does it make him psychologically happier as it does wives but physiologically happier too. Let me show you why.

TESTOSTERONE-OXYTOCIN CYCLE

In our chapter on the gendered brain, differences between the structure of male and female brains were discussed. The connections and structural differences alone begin to illuminate how relationships are impacted. Our relationships are further impacted by hormonal differences as well. Of those numerous male and female hormones we will focus on two of the heaviest hitters—testosterone and oxytocin.

Testosterone is the male sex hormone. While also found in females, males produce significantly more of it. Testosterone affects behavior, mood, and the male sex circuits, but is also associated with male aggressiveness, competitiveness, and assertiveness; High testosterone levels equal high energy and a higher need for independence. And while most are familiar with this hormone, few are familiar with its female counterpart oxytocin.

Oxytocin is known as the "cuddle" hormone as it's released with hugging and cuddling. It increases sensitivity to touch and feelings of bonding for both men and women but more so in women. Oxytocin stimulates the desire to "tend and befriend," which is why women more so than men enjoy connecting with others for friendship and conversation but also find it more pleasurable to care for others by tending to their needs. It is oxytocin that is responsible for a parent's increased nurturing feelings toward a child. Lastly, increased levels of oxytocin equals increased empathy and decreased aggression as well as increased sexual receptivity in women.

But what do these hormones have to do with Superness?

Let me begin by telling you of the value of testosterone in a man's daily life. When men go to work they spend testosterone.

Whether his work is running heavy equipment on a construction site, running a department in an office building, or running computer programs in a quiet office of one, a man is busy spending this very powerful and necessary hormone. Testosterone is a man's happy hormone. The more of it he has, the more energy he has to solve, fix, build, care, create, etc. But at the end of a man's workday his testosterone is often depleted and needs to be recharged. How does he do this?

By doing nothing.

Absolutely nothing.

Tuning out.

Zoning.

In our chapter on communication we made the analogy of a man's brain to that of having different "compartments" or boxes, one for every different area of a man's life such as the kids, the finances, sex, job, etc. However, there is one more box that we had not yet discussed and that is one that author, speaker and Marriage and Family expert Mark Gungor humorously calls "The Nothing Box" and, according to Gungor, it's a man's favorite place to be (video, 2013). While no true "boxes" exist in a man's brain, the analogy serves well as a clear picture of how men store and retrieve information. Additionally, this imagery will help to illuminate the influence of testosterone in a man's marriage and on his stress (no gentlemen, marriage and stress are *not* the same thing).

Imagine it this way. When a man comes home after a long day of spending his testosterone he needs to replenish it by going to his "nothing box" and doing nothing at all—nothing that requires thinking, that is. Men need to turn off their brains. The most astounding piece of information to me and every woman I've ever delivered a seminar to is that men have the ability to turn off their brains. Men can absolutely think about nothing at all. They can stare at a TV and think about nothing. No thoughts. No commercials. They can play a video game or work out or do any of a number of things that require little more than habitual muscle memory and need not engage a single brain cell. There is not a woman in this world who doesn't wish she had that same ability because women's brains simply cannot turn off. I find, too, that many men are surprised to learn that no matter what a woman is doing her brain is always working, always making connections. Sorry guys. Women cannot stop thinking. Remember that corpus callosum that women have more of than men? Yeah, that's the culprit. When a man is able to go to and stay in his nothing box for enough time he is able to begin functioning anew. But much like a car's gas tank, the less time he has to recharge the less energy he'll be able to regain. Often though, a man's ability to recharge is inhibited and it's often by his woman who has no idea she is doing so because she recharges in an entirely different way—by building her oxytocin.

For women to rebuild their oxytocin they must do anything but sit still and do nothing. They must tend and befriend. Tend to the kids, tend to the house, tend to her nails, the dog, the finances, tend to whatever needs tending. Once it's taken care of and her honey-do list is empty only then can she relax. Every guy reading this just sighed a mutual Ugh. *No wonder she never relaxes and always bugs me to get these menial tasks over with! She can't de-stress until they are done! My life is over!*

And that tending includes talking to you. *Hi honey, how was your day? Did you get that project done? What did your boss say? Did he appreciate it? I would have. I know how hard you worked on it. Let me tell you all about my day. So today when Sally came in and I showed her my project...* You get the picture. But guys, when women do this oxytocin-induced question and answer session she has no idea that she is short-circuiting the very testosterone-building you need in order to be there for her mentally and emotionally. For men to recharge they need to do nothing. For women to recharge they need to do anything *but* nothing. The more she talks to him and tries to connect the more testosterone he's spending. The more he spends the less energy he has. The less energy he has the less he does for her and the more upset or hurt she gets. The less loved she feels. It's a bad cycle and one that many couples find themselves in. So what do we do?

First of all, we allow each other to recharge. I usually instruct the ladies to give her husband the first half hour of the day when he gets home to do nothing. Don't talk to him unless he initiates it. While doing so I instruct the women to spend the time building oxytocin by tending to their own or someone else's needs. Call a girlfriend or play with the kids, etc. Once a man has had ample time to recharge he will usually be able to (and should) help you build more oxytocin by helping out in those ways you need him to most. In doing so, the needs of both are being met and both are a bit happier. But for men this goes one step further that enhances your energy and marital happiness in ways unavailable to women—by selflessly serving her.

Science has shown that when a man pleases his wife *and believes that he is the source of her happiness* his testosterone goes up. When his testosterone goes up he has more energy to do those things that please her most: hang the blinds, go for a walk with her, play with the kids. When he does those things *and* he sees his wife's appreciation his testosterone goes up. His wife-centered actions make her feel loved and her oxytocin goes up. When her oxytocin goes up she is happier. When she is happier she is more likely to express that happiness to her husband. When she expresses that happiness to her husband his testosterone again goes up and he again has more energy to please her. It's a beautiful cycle.

But this is key: in order for the cycle to work a husband must actually see the fruits of his labor in his wife's expression of happiness or appreciation. Often times that does not take place and a man feels, rather, that no matter what he does for his wife she is never happy. Rather than thanking him for hanging the blinds she may add a comment that minimizes the action instead "Well, I asked you to hang them three weeks ago. It's about time you did so." When this lack of appreciation is expressed, though the task has been completed, the husband receives no extra boost of testosterone and his levels are actually lowered. He is deflated and has less energy to do anything else off of his wife's To-Do list and neither spouse benefits.

But imagine if every time wives positively witness their husbands' efforts they extend their appreciation. Men would continually have their energy renewed thus allowing for the potential to serve their wives further. And they'd be happier—both the wives *and* the husbands.

I was always irritated by the phrase "happy wife, happy life" because it created for me an image that made women look more selfish than men. But the science regarding the testosterone-oxytocin cycle illuminates the truth behind this phrase. But why? Wouldn't the reverse be true? Happy husband, happy life?

No.

And this is why.

When women serve their husbands they receive no additional oxytocin benefits. Our oxytocin levels remain the same. You could love him, serve him and please him all day and despite that oxytocin stores would receive no boost.

This knowledge regarding the testosterone-oxytocin cycle does not negate a woman's need for marital selflessness if she desires an extremely happy marriage. Our chapter on happiness already showed that putting another's needs before our own is the surest way to happiness. This current explanation illuminates the *added* benefits to men for their selfless service to their wives. Super Couples make this cycle habitual. This research makes *primary* the Super Husband's role in an extremely happy marriage. Super is easier to attain if a husband is Super first—if he first places his wife's needs *before* his own. But this cycle will be rendered inept if wives do not fulfill their role in the cycle of recognizing and appreciating all he has done and continues to do for her. The more he pleases her, the more she appreciates him. The more she shows him she appreciates him the more his testosterone increases. The more his testosterone increases the happier he is and the more energy and desire he has to please her again. Testosterone is a physiological reward for selflessness. The testosterone-oxytocin cycle is selflessness at its best.

To think that selflessness begets happiness in both the giver and the receiver illuminates a beautiful model for any marriage. Super marriages are born out of selfless submission to one's spouse. 'Til death do they part, the Super Husband's sole responsibility is to seek daily to meet his wife's needs *foremost* and it is her responsibility to seek to meet his.

Daily.

But there is one more extremely important gendered aspect of selflessness that must be addressed before super can be attained: the relationship between love and sex.

LOVE AND SEX

Love and sex are arguably two of the most talked about topics in our society today—okay, not just today, maybe since Adam and Eve arrived in Eden. But their connection differs, for the most part, based on whether we are male or female.

For the majority of men, (ladies, pay attention) love and sex are nearly the same thing. I love you therefore I want to have sex with you. You love me therefore you should want to have sex with me. Let me stop right here and clarify that I am not saying that any time a man has sex with a woman he believes he loves her. The statement is ludicrous in this highly over-sexualized hook-up culture that mocks virginity and esteems sexual freedom and conquest. What I am referring to is sex within the marital relationship where the couple has professed their love for one another and accepts sex as a natural reflection of that love. But within the bounds of Holy Matrimony where the two are intricately related, that relationship is affected by gender. Because for most men, sex and love are nearly synonymous; it is difficult for most husbands to understand how or why their wives cannot desire sex or, worse yet, refuse it. Though this next statement may seem crazy to its female readers, nearly every man in my marriage seminars has affirmed its accuracy. Because men can only with great difficulty separate their desire for love from their desire for sex they often believe (somewhat subconsciously) one of two things: A) if my wife doesn't want to have sex with me she no longer loves me or B) she must be having it with someone else. The women are equally as astounded as I used to be as this statement, to women, seems nothing short of ridiculous. *What? Just because I didn't want to have sex with you, you think I don't love you? I didn't want sex because I was tired, or I was busy, or I had a project that needed completion, or I wanted to watch Dancing with the Stars.* You know, important stuff.

Though I make light of it, I must assure you that women, like men, desire and enjoy sex too—evidenced by the great frequency with which they had it when they first got together (or got married). Of course we've already learned the male brain lights up two hundred and fifty percent more frequently for sex than does the female's brain, but this current explanation pertains not to sexual frequency but rather its relationship with the feeling of love. Men need sex in order to show love or feel loved.

Women are different. I know. News flash. For women, sex is the byproduct of having *felt* loved. Make her feel loved and she'll want to have sex. *You cleaned up the kids, you told me I was beautiful, you made dinner though you were exhausted, you sat with me and chatted about your day, you texted me for no reason that I was special to you...you made me feel loved, you made me feel loved, you made me feel loved. Oh my gosh, honey I love you so much I want to make love to you!*

Men often confuse affection with foreplay. They are very different. In my seminars I pose the question "What is the difference between sex and affection? To which I answer "One you can do in front of your parents. The other you cannot. One you should have been doing on your first date. The other you better have not." Affection has little to do with sex. Though one often leads to the other, neither is necessary to have the other. Everyone understands what sex is because it is tangible and easily defined. Affection is more abstract and looks different from person to person. While affection includes hugging, cuddling, and touch that can lead to sex it also includes nonsexual touch, like massages, hand holding and other gentle physical gestures. However, affection also includes those things that to many men have zero to do with sex in their minds such as the aforementioned examples of bathing the kids, cleaning the toilets for a wife who hates cleaning toilets, midday calls and texts just to remind her she's on your mind. Don't laugh men, but for affection-craving women these can all be extremely arousing. *Huh? What? But we're not even naked!*

While I could write an entire book on this topic alone, the purpose of this conversation is to show the connection between these two beautiful products of a Super marriage and their relationship to selflessness. Whether you are the one who desires sex more often in your relationship or affection the problem is this: if we do not make our spouse's sexual or affection needs a priority we'll get neither—and the love will follow.

Ladies, if you knew your husbands' needs for sex were so physiologically powerful that refusal to make love to him left him feeling utterly frustrated, unloved, unappreciated or disrespected would you desire to make love to him more often? It is my hope your answer is yes. But I must warn you that a man who believes his wife is only having sex with him out of obligation would rather hear fingers down a chalkboard than to feel so emasculated and undesired. It is a huge turnoff. Remember, sex and love are intertwined for men. While in many marriages sex is often withheld or used as a tool to be manipulated, in Super marriages it is not.

Sex within Super marriages is as personal and diverse as in all other marriages. It's unique to its couple in frequency and kind. Like other couples, sixty-six percent of Super Wives prefer sex less often than do their husbands. But as exemplified earlier, the Super Wife desires to meet the sexual needs of her husband because it makes him happy—a physical act of selfless giving. But in Super marriages selflessness is reciprocal.

Keeping this in mind I'd like to pose a question to the men. Could you have sex without being aroused? Absolutely not. Yet women are consistently expected to do that. How would you feel about expecting your wife to have sex with you if you knew she didn't feel loved by you? That's exactly what happens for a woman who did not first receive affection from you. Men must be physically aroused. Women must be emotionally aroused. But often that does not take place. In many marriages a wife often feels as if *she* is not desired by her husband but only *sex* is. She just happens to be the only option allowable to meet that need. Forgive my crassness, but many a woman has expressed that she feels like nothing more than a piece of meat, or an object to be used at her husband's desire. *"He doesn't desire me! He just wants sex."* For these women sex is not seen as a means for her husband to express his love but rather to meet his physiological need. This draws her further from and not closer to her husband. As I understand the hurtful potential of the prior statement it is my belief that most husbands want nothing more than to please their wives sexually and would be devastated if they believed their wives felt anything less than loved. But husbands, many of you are missing the mark. Whether or not you're cognizant of it, it is *your responsibility alone* to arouse your wives—just as you did when you were first trying to win her heart and succeeded. But do not feel discouraged because you are just as capable of this today as you were the first day of your marriage. Allow me now an analogy to clarify and remedy this problem from taking place in your marriage.

THE WIFE BOX

Consider our conversation on the male brain's "compartmentalization." Remember that male brains are designed to be singularly focused. When focused on a topic his brain goes to that compartment or "box" that deals with that topic: the career box, the budget box, the kid box, the sex box. However, there is one more box in the male brain we have not yet discussed—the "wife" box.

In our chapter on love we discussed being made to feel the center of our spouse's world. This is an extremely powerful feeling for both spouses but especially for women as it fuels their need to feel attractive, desirable, and pursued. Based on hormonal differences, men have a greater need for competition and conquering. While dating, he made his singular focus "conquering the heart" of the object of his affection—his future wife. *I want to marry this amazing woman and I will do all*

I can to win her heart. Of course, the first thing he wanted to do once he won her heart was to make love to her but that made winning her hand in marriage all the more thrilling and desirable. As such, he went immediately to his "wife box." She liked flowers, he bought six dozen. She liked conversation, so he talked with her through the wee hours of the night. She liked skiing, he learned to ski. Whatever it took to show her he loved and desired her he did. And it worked.

Here's the problem. Once the male has won the prize he "checks" the box and contentedly moves on to the next challenge that needs conquering: the career, buying a house, earning a degree. In doing so he necessarily moves out of the "wife box" and into the next. And while she understands he must do those things for a time, she stops feeling desired. Though she may not necessarily feel he's as focused on her as he once was, in the early years of marriage she may overlook this for a time trusting he still loves her and doing all she can to love him back, which includes making love to him even if she does not feel loved. Eventually, this takes a toll on her and she feels sex is more desired than she is. What she perceives is her husband's focus on the sex box—with no focus on the wife box.

Husbands, when your focus is on pursuing sex and not on pursuing your wife you will lose both. However, shift your focus back to winning your wife and you gain both.

Women's hearts must be won over each and every day—for the rest of your life. To be a Super Husband you must submit your needs for sex to her needs for affection and anything else it takes to make her feel desired and central to your world. But remember, true happiness is gained when we seek first to please our spouses. Selflessness is an integral part of the sexual relationship just as it is in every other part of the marriage. While a husband should selflessly seek daily to go to his "wife box" a wife should likewise focus on his needs—sexual or otherwise.

When striving toward a Super marriage, selflessness is the first step. While not our first nature, selflessness can soon become second nature in our marriages. But it *must* be practiced daily. So how do we do this? If we are to learn from Super Couples, what comes next is to rely on perception.

SC PRINCIPLE #2: ATTENTIVENESS
LOVE DOES NOT KEEP RECORD OF WRONGS...

It may surprise you to know that not all Super Couples allow me the privilege of an interview. I understand that because the unknown is uncomfortable for most people. Though I do my best to put couples at ease by explaining what the interview will look like, many are still apprehensive. Though I've faced this with a good portion of the couples I never fully understood their fear until I interviewed Lisa and Chad. We had a lot of fun joking around because Chad is definitely gifted with a sense of humor. At the interview's end Lisa stated that this wasn't bad at all. But her next statement revealed to me not only what made other Super Couples apprehensive but also another reason for their successful marriages. Lisa said, "I was afraid you'd make us open up the boxes."

Having never heard this before I asked her to explain. "Well, when we have a disagreement or are upset with each other there comes a point when we recognize our fight could go one of two directions and only one of them is good." She continued by explaining that when they are upset with each other they have two choices: they could hold onto their perspective and not let go of it until they got their spouse to change his/her mind or, worse so they'd have ammunition to use against their spouse during a future fight. As she continued, Lisa expressed that few arguments are worth holding onto and that if she wanted to remain happy with Chad she decided it was more important to take that issue, shut it in a box with no intention to retrieve it again. To be clear, Lisa was not advocating ignoring problematic issues that needed resolution—conflict avoidance—but rather assessing issues and deciding which were and were not detrimental to marital happiness. "Most of the time," Lisa stated "I realized Chad was more important to me than winning the argument so I'd put the issue in a box, put it high on a shelf and let it go."

Lisa's initial fear that I would make her "open the boxes" was a wise decision employed to protect the integrity of the marriage. She did not want to revisit unproductive issues that would not draw her closer to Chad. Her habitual focus was on those areas that drew them together.

It became apparent that not "opening the boxes" was a trait all Super Couples employed in some manner. At its core, this strategy is one in which individuals consciously *choose* to pay attention to some details, situations, or traits and ignore others. They choose to see their spouse or an issue from a perspective that will only edify the marriage. From this interviewer's perspective it was the very reason Super Couples had a veritable inability to recall past fights or disagreements they'd experienced throughout the course of their marriage. Most could only recall one or two relatively innocuous issues that had taken place decades past such as one husband's having forgotten to come home with his wife's requested ice cream during an extremely emotional day of pregnancy or another couple's long past argument after an announced visit from the in-laws that forced a last minute change of vacation plans. Though today the couples laughed about it, it revealed that though the issues had once been heated enough to have been recalled twenty years later (under interviewer pressure), that the couples had rendered the issues powerless to divide them by choosing to pay more attention to the positive qualities of their spouse and perceive negatively only *situations*—not their spouses. As such, this interviewer noticed, and will now devote the following chapter to one very powerful aspect of attentiveness.

PERCEPTION

The details we pay attention to affect how we perceive that same object, person, or situation. Have you ever heard the saying that there are always three sides to every story: mine, yours, and the truth? Perception is a funny thing. Nearly all of us want to believe our perception of a situation or person are most accurate—that the way that *I* am seeing things is at least ninety percent accurate to the ways things really are—and that if there are any discrepancies it is a problem with *the other person's* perception. I mean, *"I was there. I saw it with my own eyes for crying out loud. I know what I saw."* I understand this because I have felt the same way myself throughout my life. However, though I want to phrase this as gently as possible, I must admit that when we have these beliefs we are exhibiting a form of arrogance in believing that of all perceptions of a particular matter *mine* are most accurate. But are they? Just as a matter of logic it would seem safe to say that part of the time my perception is more accurate and the other part yours is more accurate. Then which situations do I perceive more accurately? And which situations do you perceive more accurately? Who cares? Is perception really that big of a deal anyway?

Well, yes. But even those situations that we perceive more accurately (if we were able to judge) than another are based on those areas of our lives—our skill sets—in which we are more experienced or have more knowledge. For instance, my husband Dan as you know is an avid hunter. If he had to choose between a night sitting in a tree seeking *deer* or a night at dinner sitting next to *his dear* guess which he'd choose? (*Yeah, I know. I think I'm going to have to grow a set of antlers*). We view the world from the lens of our own interests and experiences. As such, if we were walking through a forest (becoming meals for the trillion mosquitoes that reside there) and Dan said, "A herd of deer has just passed through here within the hour" and I said "No they didn't," whose perception would you believe is more accurate? Dan's of course, since he is innately familiar with the environment and likely saw many things not at all apparent to me such as tree scrapings, patterns of broken branches, and whatever else it is that environmentalists see that non-environmentalists like me do not. However, if we are sitting in a mall, or church, or any other public place people watching I'm suggesting you might want to choose my perception of the person's current emotional states and behaviors over Dan's. I'm really good at it. Have I mentioned I teach university-level communication classes? I am expert at reading people's facial expressions and body language to quite a high degree of accuracy.

For several years I remember clearly observing a particular couple in church that I was certain was headed for divorce. They sat right across from us for well over a year and my husband not only never noticed them, once I pointed them out he had to be instructed as to why I believed this couple was extremely unhappy and heading toward divorce court. For instance, though they stood next to each other there was always space in between their bodies—no touching allowed. Both would face forward statue-like with only the expression of anger or disgust on their faces. The husband looked especially disgusted. Neither would smile, neither would move their hands from the closed positions in front of their abdomens and, when preparing to sit, they would most certainly never turn their bodies inward toward each other for even the brief moment it took to reach behind them for their seats. Both would look toward their outer shoulders furthest away from his/her spouse so as not to accidentally have any intimate eye contact with the other. I could detail all of the behaviors noted but suffice it to say eventually I no longer saw them in church. After doing some reconnaissance I was told that "Mr. and Mrs. Unhappy" had gotten divorced. Though extremely sad to see any couple divorce it affirmed my perceptions were correct. I had observed as accurately a situation in an area of my expertise as did Dan in the forest.

So perception, though partial and flawed, is a huge factor in how we relate interpersonally with others and our world, especially as it relates to the marital relationship and of course the Super Couple. Consider this, if you and I were to look at the same object—an apple for instance—most people would assume we are both "seeing" the same thing in exactly the same way: its shape, color, height, and imperfections. But are we? For instance, if we are both facing each other with the apple between us we are each seeing a different side of the apple. What if there is a bruise or a worm hole on my side but your side looks flawless? What then? Aren't our perceptions of the deliciousness or edibility of that apple going to differ greatly? What if we try to account for the potential of this taking place and, in an attempt to minimize differences in perception, actually go around the circumference of the apple with our eyes to observe what the other observed? Wouldn't that then be sufficient to assume we had perceived the object in the same way? It would be an improvement, certainly, but absolutely insufficient. What if one of us was color blind? How then could we both see the apple in the same way? Further, what if I didn't *know* I was color blind? What if both of us held this apple, smelled it and then even cut it open and ate a slice of it? Would our perceptions now be more similar or dissimilar? After all, we're both experiencing this same apple at the same time in the same way. Clearly we must both feel the same way about it. But we don't. I might now say, "this apple is the sweetest apple I have ever eaten" while you might say, "this apple is sour." How could this happen? Well it's simple: we both have different sets of taste buds. Mine might be more sensitive than yours and thus pick up nuances of the apple that may totally escape your notice like my sommelier friend Crystal whose taste buds are so sensitive she can pick out the type of barrel a wine was fermented in just from its flavor residue in the wine—oak perhaps—while I'm thinking *Are you serious? All I can tell from this sip is that it's red, it's sweet, and that I want another.* Had Crystal and I both bitten into the same apple she surely would have been more sensitive to its nuances than I would have been because my taste buds are simply not as sensitive as hers.

Second, even if we are medically tested and found to have the same exact taste buds with the same exact sensitivities, we cannot both possibly eat the same exact slice of the apple. We might eat the slices that are adjacent to one another but even then they are still two wholly separate and unique slices. Whose perception of the apple is correct then? Well, both. What I perceived was truth to me just as what you perceived was truth to you. The problem occurs when I *value* my perception alone as accurate and disregard yours as flawed. Can't both of our perceptions be correct to some degree? After all, a person wouldn't lie about something so insignificant. For whatever reason, his apple tasted much differently to him than mine did to me. Both are correct. I must just decide when it is important enough to argue about or to let it go and "put it in a box."

Like our tastes, our perceptions of people can also change over time. Based on a greater collection of experiences, mistakes, and wisdom garnered we can look backwards and realize that how we perceived a situation twenty years ago was much different than how we'd perceive that same situation today. Persons too, are perceived differently over time. There are several people from our high school years that we never associated with that now are some of our closest friends because we see them differently. What we perceived as stuck-up in 1983 is now perceived as introversion. As I look back fifty years past, I see numerous situations differently than I did back then. My perception has changed though the situations have not.

Let's humanize this argument with a more relevant example—pain tolerance. In my decades of work I have almost never called in sick and I only once missed any school for sickness. If I got a cold or flu I was not bothered by it. I would still do what I needed to do albeit with a box of tissues at my side. I am what you'd call a suck-it-up-and-keep-going kind of girl so it never made sense to me that people would complain when they caught a cold.

Now forgive me for sounding so uncompassionate. I wasn't. I was just young. I didn't want to see anyone suffer. I still don't. It's just that based on *my* perception—since I, too, had experienced colds and flus and thus was a veritable expert on them—these people clearly had low pain tolerance. But see, this is why perception is such a defining part of experience. Like that slice of apple, how did I know we were both actually *feeling* the same effects of the cold? What if we were each experiencing different cold strains? What if God himself came down and told us they were the very same cold germs and the very same cold symptoms? What then? What other factors might be at play? You see, perception of how another is experiencing the very same situation is much like looking at that apple from different sides or even tasting adjacent slices. There are always other unknown but contributing factors that influence how we perceive the various situations and interactions in our lives. Like the persons with differing taste bud sensitivities, what if we had differing nerve sensitivities causing one to feel more strongly the cold symptoms and another person to feel very little of them at all? What if we have fewer or more nerve endings than another? What if our nerve endings were closer to our skin surface than the nerve endings of another? Do those people who seem to be complaining about some physical ailment have a lower pain tolerance or are they actually feeling much more of the pain than I do?

Perception is formed based on the perspective from which one is looking and it will nearly always differ when viewed with different lenses. In each of these examples we are dealing with the same thing: two people seeing the same object or scenario in two very divergent ways. So what is this all about?

Perception is a funny thing. Like our attempt to study the apple using every sense available, no matter what we do we cannot control for internal differences or past experiences of the other perceivers. It is actually commendable of the one who sought to minimize perception differences as much as possible by trying to see all of its sides—we should do this every time we have a difference in opinion and certainly in all of our relationships. But no matter how skilled we are as perceivers, there will be nonetheless other factors beyond our comprehension and no two people will ever perceive that apple or cold in exactly the same way. But do not lose hope for it is this very difference in perception and striving to minimize those differences that can serve to improve relationships and draw people closer to one another. Choosing to see another person in the most positive light possible is an essential element of the Super Couple formula for it communicates a respect for the other person's perspectives as well as a willingness to self-correct when necessary for the sake of the relationship. To best explain this perceptive giving and receiving let us turn now to a tool created for that purpose—the Johari Window.

THE JOHARI WINDOW

In 1955 Joseph Luft and Harrington Ingham created the Johari Window to help people better understand themselves and their relationship with others. Used extensively in self-help groups and corporate settings, I use it to illustrate the value of perception in a Super marriage. The Johari Window divides the self into four quadrants labeled *Open, Hidden, Blind,* and *Unknown.*

The *Open* Quadrant

In the first quadrant are the parts of myself that are both "known to me and known to others." Having never met me but know only what's written in this book, there are already many things that fit into this *Open* quadrant: you know I am married, I have two daughters, four perfect grandchildren, you know I have my doctorate, had a troubled marriage, love to write, that I teach marriage seminars, etc. There are numerous things we humans have no problem being open about, but most of those things are, for the most part, superficial things. They are pieces of information we believe to be *safe* enough to share with others without them getting too close to us. These are those pieces of ourselves that we usually share on a first date—or before. When we sign up for an online dating service we're asked to answer numerous questions about ourselves to help the other know enough to decide whether or not to connect further. What each of us considers information safe enough to share openly with people we just met for the first time or only a few times differs greatly from person to person.

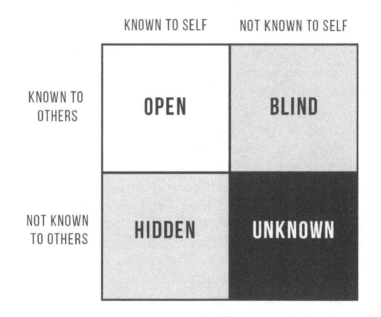

Much of what I shared already is information many would keep hidden for months or years or even forever. I have few secrets. I often joke that I should go into politics because the notoriously brutal media would find no skeletons in my closet. They're all hanging on the front door. My husband, on the other hand, pretty much doesn't want to tell people anything more than his first name, that he loves hunting, and that he is a Green Bay Packer fan. Even that might be a stretch. He may stop at "Hey, my name is Dan and that's all you need to know." Anything beyond that is private to him and thus he keeps it hidden from most. My point is that Dan and I are both comfortable with different levels of self-disclosure and for various reasons. Dan is generally more of a pessimist and is much more suspicious of others' intentions than I am. Not that this is necessarily bad, because there are a lot of con artists out there willing to take advantage of every one possible. Thus, he is cautious and feels if information is not shared it cannot be used against him, which is absolutely true. But one's spouse is not usually a con artist or one from whom we should hide ourselves. We'll readdress this later when we discuss intimacy and trust, but for now let's say that we all have differing levels of self-disclosure—pieces of information we put out into the *Open* quadrant and those pieces of information we keep hidden, which leads me to the second quadrant.

The *Hidden* Quadrant

The *Hidden* quadrant is that part of ourselves that is "known to us but unknown to others." This is where we hide those things that we are not proud of, our fears, our failings, our hurts, our desires, or anything else that we believe for some reason would either not help us if we were to share it or would definitely hurt us if others were to know of it. In this quadrant might be hidden the bankruptcy for which you filed right after college because you irresponsibly overdid it with credit cards, the fact that you've had breast implants, or any plastic surgery for that matter. In this quadrant you may hide the fact that you once were fired from your job, have an addiction to painkillers or pornography, or anything else for that matter. You might also hide your fear of dying or your fear of failure. You might hide your fear of being left alone or abandoned and you might hide your fear of rejection. Though it may sound like we are making a conscious choice to "hide" this information or feelings, be aware that those things hidden in this quadrant are not always obvious to their hiders either. In this quadrant we hide the many feelings that we are simply uncomfortable sharing: our feelings of inadequacy, incompetence, fear, loneliness, or any other feeling I do not want to share with the outer world. Also hidden in this quadrant are those thoughts you've had (good or bad) that you might be too embarrassed to share. Who wants to share the lustful thoughts they've had about another person? Or thoughts they have about their neighbors or your bad taste?

I remember when my first grade teacher asked us to name someone famous we "liked" or wanted to meet. Most of my six-year-old classmates named a member of the Brady Bunch, Partridge family, the Jackson Five, or the Osmond Brothers or any other teenaged star of the day (I know, I am totally aging myself). When she got to me I said "Dr. Welby" who was, to this first grader, about a hundred-year-old character in the TV series *Marcus Welby, M.D.* and all of a sudden the entire class broke out into laughter. Here it is nearly a half a century later and I still remember the feelings of embarrassment experienced that day because they were so powerful. For some reason I am well able to express my emotions, which is the first step in dealing with painful emotions. But many people are not so expressive and would, from that moment forward, hide deeply that experience from others to ensure they never experience again those feelings. *I will not allow myself to get laughed at again for that or any other stupid comment.* As a result, this person will begin to withhold many other valuable or intimate thoughts from conversations just in case they are perceived as stupid by our world of others.

Amazing, isn't it? One hurt can cut so deeply that it can cause us to choose to shut down or conceal a very large part of ourselves from that day forward. Additionally, this often creates an issue to be dealt with by one's future spouse as he/she has to spend significant time and energy trying to convince you he/she is a safe person with which to share your hurts without fear of retribution, laughter, or a reliving of those earlier feelings brought on by the painful incident. This is always easier said than done. For some, the hurts cut so deeply that the information goes with them to their grave. And that is saddening as it impeded a lifetime of love, joy, and intimacy from entering into the space held captive by these memories or incidents.

But all things we choose to hide in this quadrant are not necessarily bad or negative either. Many people prefer to hide their life dreams and goals as well. After all, if I tell people that I want to be a congresswoman, astronaut, or poet, or that I would love to bike across America or swim the English Channel they may laugh and tell me I'm being ridiculous and therefore discourage my aspirations. It might not even be such a grandiose dream that someone hides either but rather, for they may keep deeply hidden their dream to become the first person in their family to graduate from high school or college. It might seem strange if you've come from a healthy family, but many from abusive or dysfunctional families have to fight their own families' perceptions that "you are never going amount to anything" or, even if they feel you *are* going to amount to something, some goals are considered too high and they are counseled by "wise" adults to be more realistic and aspire to do something more attainable. Expressing a goal like this might create such an insurmountable amount of opposition or stress that the individual chooses, rather, to hide it in the *Hidden* quadrant. I recently watched the movie *Silver Linings Playbook* in which the main character hid from his family and friends the fact that he was practicing for an upcoming dance contest. Even though he was working toward something positive, he was not prepared to accept the taunting he'd likely receive once others found out. So the goal remained hidden (for a while).

Many well-intentioned others will, for various reasons, stymie our success if we let them in too far. This exemplifies why not only negative experiences, thoughts and feelings are in our *Hidden* quadrants but also positive ambitions, thoughts and experiences as well.

The *Blind* Quadrant

The third quadrant identified by Luft and Harrington is labeled the *Blind* quadrant. This is the part of ourselves that is "unknown to me but known to others." At first glance one might say "Huh? What can you possibly know about me that I don't?" The easiest way to understand this quadrant is to consider the alcoholic. Isn't it true that most of the time others are clearly aware that one close to them is an alcoholic before that person sees it himself?

I was teaching a series of leadership seminars to a group of high-ranking civilian and military executives and one of the students—a fiftyish male of relatively high corporate status—asked me to do some marriage mentoring for him and his wife. He said he definitely respected my ways of seeing the world, and respected my opinions and skills. Clearly, because I was so good at getting others to communicate more effectively, work through conflict and build rapport, he was certain I could help him and his wife as well. Though we began our sessions as a one-on-one between him and me, I began to suspect one particular issue he was skirting because of the phraseology he used in describing the couple's issues. Later that week I met his wife for the first time and after less than an hour of speaking with her my suspicions that he was an alcoholic were confirmed. And not just a slight alcoholic but a "multi-millionaire, fly around the world, hire prostitutes and escorts, and accidentally pocket call my wife sloppy drunk because I am too oblivious to control my actions" kind of alcoholic. The next time he and I met he asked if I were able to talk some sense into his wife and get her to "stop complaining" so much so that they could once again be happily married. When I started to address his drinking problem he respectfully told me I had no idea what I was talking about and that he was mistaken when he thought I would be different from the other persons he had sought help from in the past. He couldn't understand why I, his pastor, and a slew of friends, colleagues, and counselors constantly kept getting on him about his drinking when he had a marriage in crisis that we needed to focus on.

This is the essence of the *Blind* quadrant and exemplifies precisely why we are blind to a large portion of ourselves. Certainly, the above example was a radically obvious one to make the point that there are parts of ourselves that others know about us and we are oblivious to. Not everything in this quadrant is quite as obvious to those around us or detrimental to our self-revelation and intimate relationships. I recently conducted a pre-marital seminar and my mother, who was visiting from out of town, came with me to observe. Four hours later, my mom couldn't help but point out that I habitually tuck my hair behind my left ear so often that it annoyed her. Thanks Mom. I'm glad you noticed such a profoundly important aspect of my presentation. No offense taken. But this is the *Blind* quadrant. In this quadrant we find not only our habits but where others recognize our patterns of behavior before we recognize them ourselves—that which we are blind to.

Have you ever had to pull a friend aside in order to "speak the truth in love" to her? I have. But I have also been that friend pulled aside too. I can remember a very painful situation where some close friends of mine pulled me aside and told me something about myself that was very difficult to hear. I went home. I cried. I thought about their words and then I had a choice to make. I could choose to think that these four people were mistaken or mean or didn't really love me or I could choose to accept that what they had to say was true—at least in part—and then make a decision to act on that new information or not. I had a teacher in high school who did something similar. I'll never forget it. Erico was both my Spanish teacher and one of my music directors. I just loved Erico—we all did. I was seventeen when he handed me a handwritten letter one day after school. On the outside it read "Private. For your eyes only" and I had no idea of its contents. The contents were painful to read as he expressed to me a perceived character flaw that he was no longer going to tolerate.

That letter obviously changed my life—proof of which is shown in my having kept it these three decades later. I didn't keep it because it made me feel good about myself but rather the opposite. It hurt me deeply. I cried the entire time I read it and, further, I never told a single other person about that letter (and I usually told my friends everything) until decades later when I accidentally stumbled upon it. I felt so embarrassed that I didn't know how I would face him the next day at school. I wished I could hide under a rock because before reading it I felt great about myself, but now I felt naked. I kept Erico's letter because I knew (or *chose* to believe—and we do have a choice) that Erico's true intentions were not to hurt me but to help me to become the best version of myself possible. He saw potential in me but he also saw how my negative traits and decisions were hurting that potential. I'm happy to say I took Erico's comments to heart and, after some soul searching recognized that what Erico said was correct. He had seen something in me that I was blind to. But therein lays the challenge associated with this *Blind* quadrant: we are unable to completely learn about ourselves apart from the "sight" of others. But the good news is that once the information is made known to us and we are not blind to it (whether we like it or not) it shifts to either our *Open* quadrant as I just did or at least to our *Hidden* quadrant ("I know this about myself but I am uncomfortable exposing it to others). Actually, there is a third place for that new self-knowledge to go and that may be— in the case of negative traits—to disappear completely because we have deliberately trained these bad habits or qualities away. You see, once we are aware of this information we are able to do something about it. In both of the cases I referenced above, the letter from Erico or the intervention of my four friends, I was able to take that new self-knowledge and fix those parts of myself that I felt needed improving. As for the hair tucking situation...Mom is going to have to deal. I've got more important bad habits to work on.

But remember, though my friends saw me from a different perspective than I saw myself, they still only saw me incompletely. They could never see me from the same perspective from which I saw myself, because only I had fully walked every mile of my personal journey. Others only journeyed with me for *portions* of that journey. Others help us fill in the blanks or blind spots of our lives and those most intimate with us—such as our mothers— see a more complete version of us than do those less intimate, though they, too, still only see a part of us.

The *Unknown* Quadrant

But there is a final quadrant known as the *Unknown* quadrant, which, as the name implies, is that part of myself that is neither known to me nor known to others, yet. This important part of ourselves is what propels our life's journey: self-discovery. As we age and go through life gathering memories, experiences, knowledge, and wisdom this quadrant shrinks—or at least should. Most likely you know more about yourself today than you knew yesterday. Granted, some of us pay more conscious attention to self-discovery than do others, but unless we are comatose we are learning about ourselves each and every day just like I now know that I apparently tuck my hair behind my left ear too much, or that I am good at making people comfortable in embarrassing situations, or that I sometimes cut people off when they are speaking without letting them finish their thoughts, or that I am considered funny or even quick-witted sometimes. While none of us will ever know ourselves perfectly, our unspoken goal in life is to shrink this quadrant to as small as possible. But herein lays the purpose of perception: *it is only in and through our relationships with others that we can begin to fully understand and know ourselves.* Most importantly, it is those who are most intimate with us that can best help us on this journey of self-revelation. As such, not only are our spouses best able to do so because of their daily interactions with us, but more than any other, they are *responsible* for doing so. The two shall be as one. Right? Thus helping me to be a better me will help you to be a better you and us to be a better we.

So what are we to do with all of this? For what purpose does knowing about these four quadrants of ourselves serve? Further, what does any of this have to do with Super Couples? Consider this, if my goal is to shrink my *Unknown* quadrant—to get to know myself intimately—it is essential that I begin to cultivate the practice of one very specific action because this endeavor is impossible apart from the help of another. That action is TRUST. And who better to help us along our journey of self-revelation than the one whose single most important role in marriage is to be our helpmate?

TRUST

Do you trust your boss to look out for your best interests and those of the rest of the staff? Do you trust that when the light turns red oncoming traffic will actually stop? Do you trust that when you open up a can that's marked "Peas" on the outside that you will actually find peas inside? Do you trust that when you tell the barista "nonfat, decaf, latte" that your drink will, in fact, be all of those things? I trust mine. But there have been occasions where twenty minutes post beverage I find myself talking a pace significantly quicker than my usual one thousand words per minute and I realize that my trust has, in fact, been misplaced—not intentionally mind you, but misplaced nonetheless. Trust is huge. We can't live or function without some trust in some person, some thing or some institution. But trust doesn't mean that those persons or institutions holding the trust have intentionally broken that trust on those occasions where it has been broken. My barista is human. She makes mistakes. Should I forever hold that caffeinated mistake over her head as punishment or a constant reminder of her flawed nature? Do I trust her the next time she makes my beverage or do I go to another barista and hope she, too, will never fail at this same task? As a matter of fact, in my lifetime, several baristas have accidentally given me a caffeinated beverage when what I ordered was a decaf. I can't possibly keep switching until I find one who is guaranteed never to make this mistake. Can I? Well, I can, but I would for the rest of my days on this earth need to continue to switch baristas because it will happen again. I can promise you that much.

So what is the point of this analogy?

I could continue to go to the same barista but see if this problem continues; next time maybe remind her as she's hitting buttons "Is that the decaf?" I actually have reminded my barista and since most want caffeinated beverages she often catches herself, apologizes and says it's a habit. I get that. Muscle memory is powerful. I cut her mental slack and assume she *wants* to do it right, and then continually try to guide her lovingly, respectfully, patiently, kindly...love is patient after all. Right? I can't expect change overnight. At first maybe she'll develop a way to remember I always want decaf when she sees me at least. But she may still make the mistake with others because she was extra alert with me. Quite possibly, she eventually figures out a way to ensure she rarely makes this mistake with all of her customers (develops her own mental trick). But then, maybe not. Maybe she always makes this mistake with others but at least she rarely makes it with me. Isn't that the goal after all? While this may sound selfish "Hey, I don't care how you treat others as long as you treat *me* this way," truly it's not. What it is saying is that if I am her focus or "the center of her world" for that moment she will make a more concerted effort to please me. In Super marriages we're not expecting super men and super women—people who always have it right and just struggle less. Super spouses are imperfect too. They make mistakes. The difference is that in their marriages they realize that though they can't focus on the needs of everyone in the world at all times (as that would make us crazy) their commitment is to focus on changing/improving themselves in order to best meet the needs of their spouse. In essence, that's what we're doing when we want the barista to remember *our* drink. If I was her number one favorite customer (and clearly I must be) I would have no doubt that when I walked in the door she would alter the ways she does things a bit in order to remember how it is I like to be treated.

Trust is risk.

For my *Unknown* quadrant to shrink, my *Hidden* and *Blind* quadrants must shrink as well. To do either takes both trust and risk. To shrink my *Hidden* quadrant I must risk a great deal of emotional security by trusting that the persons with whom I share these hidden parts of myself—my thoughts, feelings, dreams, mistakes, goals—will not only receive them but most importantly, protect them, cherish them, and *not* throw them in my face or use them against me. Let me give you an example of this from my own marriage. When I was a stupid young teenager my father and I did not get along. Though I am now ashamed to admit it, I used to hate my father when we would get into our fights. Over the years of marriage and numerous conversations I have obviously shared that information with my husband. In doing so this "hidden" information became known and moved into the *Open* quadrant (open to Dan at least). I trusted Dan with this information because I loved him. He was my husband. Isn't that what we're supposed to do? Well, many years later during one of our really bad fights when screaming, crying, anger, and hurt feelings were manifested (on both parts) I told my husband that I hated him. My husband then said to me something to the effect of "Well, I don't have a problem. You have the problem. You hate me like you said you used to hate your dad. Maybe you just hate everyone you don't agree with and you're the problem."

This statement cut me deeply on various levels. First, it angered me because it showed my husband was unwilling (at that time) to take any responsibility for *his* part in our marital problems or specifically, that particular argument by implying "*It's all you Christine,*" which of course is rarely the case in any conflict. Second, I had entrusted my husband with a very painful emotional and intimate piece of information about my childhood. I opened myself up to him and his potential judgment or protection and rather than protect that gift—an intimate part of his spouse—he used it as ammunition in an attack against me by throwing it back into my face at a very sensitive moment. By doing so he protected himself and left my heart open to hurt and pain. Whose needs were being met in that instance? Certainly not mine.

I will often pose the question in my seminars, "If someone threw into your face a less-than-positive piece of intimate information you entrusted with them, how likely would you be next time to share another personal piece of information with that person?" The answer is always the same: never or very unlikely. Please don't think any less of my husband for my having shared the above example for it is likely that, though I don't remember, I did the same thing to him during those painful years. But since it didn't hurt me to say them it wasn't retained in the forefront of my memory bank. Our emotional memories are at the forefront of our brains. The experiences that weren't especially emotional—positive or negative—were thus also not memorable.

I'll never forget the amazing feelings of seeing my daughter's face for the very first time on the delivery table, or the feeling when I saw the presents under the tree on Christmas morning knowing Santa had somehow snuck into our house unnoticed yet again. And I will *never, ever* forget the feelings of being trapped on the front steps of my school one day many years ago by three mean eighth grade girls (bullies in every sense of the word) when I was only six because I had a terrible lateral lisp (the kind they always make fun of in the movies where you spit all over everyone when you say any word with the letter "S" in it). The big, bossy fourteen-year-old leader of the bullies "Tammy" had called over two of her eighth-grade buddies to come listen to and laugh at me. She kept yelling at me and demanding that I say, "I want a sizzling steak smothered in sautéed onions." As I cowered below them in the fetal position in the corner of the large cement stairwell outside of the side entrance of St. Hedwig School sobbing, refusing to say it, the three bullies only drew menacingly nearer and continued to laugh hysterically and mock me, Tammy kept shouting "Say it! SAY IT!" With tears pouring endlessly down my face I kept trying to make them go away by saying things like "I can't say that." or "Stop! Go away!" "Please leave me alone!" But no matter what, I couldn't think of a single phrase that didn't include a word with the letter S in it. So I sat there sobbing until they finally walked away, bummed that they hadn't gotten me to repeat their coveted phrase, but laughing all the while. Just typing that brought back the powerful emotions that I associated with that very painful experience so many years past. Funny, isn't it? I struggle to remember the names of all of my students by the end of each semester but I can vividly recall every detail of that very emotional experience more than four decades after the ten-minute incident took place.

I walked home that day with two choices: I could share that experience with someone whom I trusted and put it out into the open or I could hide it, be hurt by it, and spend the rest of my life trying to eliminate the letter S from the English alphabet. Fortunately I chose the former. I cried as I shared all the very painful nuances of those moments with my mother whose heart also now ached at the pain her precious daughter had to endure. She hugged me and cried with me. My mother created for me what is known as a *safe emotional space*—one in which we feel safe sharing not only our superficial experiences and thoughts but our deeply personal ones as well. After making me feel better my mother told me that the next time Tammy picked on me I had permission to tell all of her friends that she still wet the bed (my mother was privy to this helpful information). I looked forward to that day that never came. But just knowing I had the emotional slingshot to defeat this eighth-grade Goliath was enough to give this first grader peace in this personal issue of a lisp where none had previously existed. Moreover, an equally positive residual effect of this terrible incident then took place as my mother hired a speech pathologist for me and my lisp eventually disappeared. What those mean girls meant for harm eventually bore very powerful positive consequences—because of a *risky* decision to trust another person with my emotional pain.

Could that decision to trust have backfired? Absolutely! Very sadly, many people do not have the same support networks as those of us raised in healthy homes and families. Had I been born to callous or uncaring parents, the sharing of that same experience could have garnered a much different response, such as, "Suck it up you sissy! What the hell are you crying about? No one even touched you and you're crying like a damn baby. Grow the hell up!"

Ouch.

I hurt deeply for the child in which a scenario like that might have ever played out. Because that child will one day become an adult, she will have become expert at locking up her emotions from others and protecting herself from potential hurt. I dealt with these people every day in my anger management classes.

We would spend weeks helping adults admit they have an anger issue and then begin the journey of attempting to unlock their feelings for the very first time and to begin to trust others by sharing them. And that can be an extremely scary thing to do.

A Super marriage is at its core a relationship of deep emotional trust. "Of all the people in the world I choose only you with whom to share the rest of my life: the good, the bad, my fears, failings, sadnesses, as well as my joys, thoughts, goofy mishaps, and gaffes. I will share with you those times I put my foot in my mouth as well as those times when my words were spot on and made me look great." Though we all want a Super marriage many of us are not willing to take the risks necessary to have one. We want all of the joys without any of the risks. I want to protect myself from you while simultaneously expecting you to draw nearer to me. Sorry, but we cannot have it both ways. In order to *have* it all, we must *risk* it all. *A Super marriage is an all-or-nothing venture.* We *must* be able to trust our spouses with the sharing of ourselves or we will never draw nearer to each other as is fully necessary for "the two to become one." It's just not possible. We might get to "happy" but we can *never* get to "Super."

A powerful example of the risk involved with entrusting one's spouse to some of the intimate information from one's *Hidden* quadrant comes from something a young bride once shared with me. Her name was Sara. Sara and Mark had been married for about two years when she shared this information with me. This was Sara's first marriage and it was Mark's second. At some point prior to their wedding Mark and Sara were discussing some painful details of Mark's first marriage when Mark confided to Sara that at the end of his marriage both he and his ex-wife had been unfaithful to one another—Mark had had an affair in his first marriage. I'd interacted with Sara frequently, as she and I were colleagues. In one of our regular conversations Sara mentioned to me that "she was keeping an eye on that husband of hers" as there was "no way in hell that she was *ever* going to tolerate him cheating on her." If Mark came home from work late she'd interrogate him about his whereabouts. She'd daily pick up his cell phone and scroll through his calls or texts just looking for anything inappropriate—even in front of him as if to say "I'm keeping my eye on you because I don't trust you." When she visited him at work and noticed this particular workplace "bimbo" hitting on him she'd get snotty and become passive-aggressive with Mark about it and remind him he'd "damn well never cheat on her" or she'd take him for everything he had—especially their kids. When Mark, who was the store manager, would come home later than planned and she knew the "bimbo" was closing too, she was especially critical about his tardiness. Mark was constantly forced to be on the defensive, assuring Sara he was not cheating, nor would he ever.

As we sat together one day discussing this topic I was compelled to address Sara's concerns and her fears of potentially enduring infidelity in her marriage.

"Sara, how does Mark treat you?"

"Really well. Why?"

"Has he ever looked at another woman inappropriately since you've been together?"

"Oh no. Not that I've noticed."

"Has he ever gone out at night without you?"

"No. He loves being with the family. If he's not at work he's usually with me and the kids playing outside or working on the house or something."

"Has he ever given you any reason whatsoever to believe that he does not love you or that he is out "looking" for anyone's affections other than yours?"

"No. But Christine, that doesn't matter. I just wouldn't be able to handle it if I ever found out he was cheating on me. There is no way in hell I would ever let him do that to our family or me. I'd leave him in a heartbeat."

While I understood Sara's deep desire to protect her heart from any potential pain, I found the most gentle but firm way to reframe her thoughts and fears. The conversation went something like this:

"Shame on you Sara."

"Huh? What do you mean?"

"Well, before you ever got married Mark gave you a rather substantial gift. He shared with you an extremely intimate detail about his former life that I am certain was not an easy thing to do. He was honest with you about one of his very intimate human flaws. He humbled himself before you with the truth when, let's face it, he could have hidden from you the information about his past affair and hoped you'd never find out. He could have lied about it. He could have done any of a number of different things to protect himself and his ego and yet he laid it all out in the open for you to see and judge. Don't you think that took a lot of guts?

"Well, yeah. I suppose."

"Sara, Mark is an imperfect human being. Just like you. He made a mistake. His mistake was having an affair but *not* in telling you about it. How would you have felt if he had never shared that with you before you got married but rather ten years later when you were already committed? How would you have felt if he'd hid it from you forever?"

"I suppose I'd have felt lied to and tricked."

"How much harder would it have been at that point to begin to trust him again?"

"Wow, geez. I don't know. I'm not sure I could ever fully trust again after that."

"Let me ask you another question. Do you think deep down Mark feared that by sharing that information with you that there was the potential that you'd change your mind about marrying him?"

"I guess so."

"But he shared it anyway. He took that risk. And guess what, his risk paid off. You married him regardless. You willingly went into your marriage with your eyes wide open to this imperfection of his. Why?"

"Well, I guess because I love him."

"So Sara, why on earth do you continue to take this piece of information he shared with you and throw it back into his face? If you keep doing so there will come a point where Mark will regret ever having told you the truth. Further, how likely do you think Mark will be in the future of sharing any of his mistakes with you if he knows your first inclination is to use them against him any chance you get?"

Sara just sat there listening finally understanding the point I was trying to make. Before she spoke I added one more thing.

"Sara, I am not saying that Mark will never have an affair

but I am also not saying that he will. He's a flawed human being and he *will* make mistakes. So will you. All I am saying is that the fact that he opened himself up to you about his infidelity in his first marriage doesn't increase those chances one little bit. If anything, his honesty would lean toward the belief that he would be less likely to do so—or he would have attempted to keep this information hidden. Doubly so, your fear of it taking place won't decrease those odds but will definitely hinder your marital joy each and every day it remains a focus of your thoughts. Marriage is risky because intimacy is risky. Intimacy is laying oneself bare for another to see and in order to have the most awesome marriage ever you must strive toward total intimacy daily. Mark was deeply intimate with you the day he shared his affair with you. He needs you to protect that information, not use it as ammunition. Over time, as he sees that he is able to share intimate information with you because you receive it in a manner that is emotionally safe, he will open up to you more and more intimately, more and more often. And you will be able to do the same."

I don't always see the metaphorical "light bulb go off" in my conversations with others but I did that day as I talked with Sara. Her response gave me great hope for their future marriage.

Sara saw it, too. "You are absolutely right, Christine. In my attempts to protect myself from my worst fears I have neglected to just be happy with this man and treasure what we have together. I can't change my past, but from now on I am going to simply give Mark the gift of my trust until and only if he does something to shake that trust."

I was so happy to hear Sara say that that I hugged her right on the spot. It has been more than nine years since that conversation and not once since have I heard Sara speak about this fear. Her behaviors toward Mark have been much more trusting as he has yet to do anything to shake that trust. I am not saying their marriage is perfect and they are still far from Super, but this decision to treasure the gift her husband has given her has had an amazingly positive effect on Sara's interactions with Mark and as such, his *Hidden* quadrant is just that much smaller while his *Open* quadrant—and Sara's heart—are that much more open.

Marriage is risky. So is trusting. But in order for "the two to become one" we must actively entrust our spouses with our intimate thoughts, emotions, decisions, dreams, and goals. So the essence of shrinking the *Hidden* quadrant is trust through *sharing*.

Paradoxically, the essence of shrinking the *Blind* quadrant is in trust through *receiving*. The risk involved in shrinking my *Blind* quadrant remains in the fact that I must risk my pride, my ego, and my perceptions of myself and be open to *receiving* from another "truths" about myself that I do not see and might not *want* to see.

Many years ago my parents volunteered with the *Lion's Club* guiding blind people on horseback through a wilderness trail. For many of these people this was one of the best parts of their week as they were to experience an activity that, without seeing guides, they would never have been able to experience. My parents were their eyes. In guiding them, my parents had to communicate what they saw because these people were unable to see it for themselves. They had to trust my parents to look out for their best intentions and their safety as they said, "turn to the right" or "duck your heads, there's a low tree branch ahead." They had to choose to willingly receive this information and use it to make better choices along their journeys.

Physical blindness, in a sense, is so much easier to deal with than personality and relational blindness because there is zero question about the blindness—all parties are cognizant that one's sight is impaired and that we can see what they cannot—especially the blind person. As such, not only is the blind person willing to accept the sight of the other but also values it. Like our physically blind friends who know they *must* trust our perspectives if they are to move through their days more effortlessly using our vision to help them overcome physical obstacles, so, too, must we trust others' perspectives to help us overcome the obstacles we are blind to like our alcoholism, habits, and faults.

Of all the quadrants, the *Blind* quadrant is arguably the hardest to shrink because we are often being asked to accept something we do not see. And if that piece of information is a critical assessment about a personality trait or an unfavorable habit we more proportionately push against accepting it as truth. I am currently working with a woman named Melanie in this very endeavor. Having recently endured a divorce from Leonard who had several times cheated on her both physically and emotionally, her perception is that the failure of the marriage was wholly due to Leonard's faults and failings. Oh, she said the obligatory "Of course I have faults. I'm not perfect. But I never did what Leonard did and that was worse than anything I could have ever done." While Melanie was sincere, all she admitted or recognized were superficial faults: I worked too much, I didn't spend as much time in the home as I could have. Yet Melanie is blind to something most everyone intimate with her sees and that is that she never admits to being wrong. Melanie cannot see that she can be very difficult to live with because her expectations of her husband (and everyone else for that matter) were extraordinarily high and simply unattainable. Further, while in the beginning of their marriage Leonard tried to do all in his power to please Melanie and meet her standards, Melanie did not notice his efforts but rather complained about what was left undone. Melanie was blind to the fact that her marriage and many of her friendships were more about taking and very little about giving. Being the baby of six siblings and the only girl, Melanie was extremely coddled while growing up. Whenever she opened her mouth everyone ran to her assistance. She was sweet and adorable and pleasant to be around. Melanie was infrequently told "no," and that created quite a problem in her adult life and marriage. Melanie still refuses to hear the word "no" to any of her expectations of others and she still refuses to believe that she had expected too much of Leonard. When others would attempt to get her to see what she was blind to, she'd lovingly and respectfully tell them they were wrong and she made no changes. "That's just *their* perspective but they just don't know this or that about me." Melanie refused to trust that others could see something in her if she did not see it too. As such, Melanie continues to experience the same problems and issues in her new relationships as she did in her marriage and cannot understand why. "Why won't they come to *my* house to date? Why do I have to go to theirs?" "They should drop all they are doing to come to my aid whenever I need them (and she believes she needs them often). Can't they see I need help? Can't they see I need to talk? Can't they stay up past their regular sleep schedule to be there for me?" Enough said.

The above example is no attack on Melanie as she is by all standards a wonderful and kind woman and fun to be around. Most everyone wants to be her friend. Her strengths are many. The above explanation was given to illuminate the essence of the "blind spot" and the difficulty in trusting others enough to receive their gift of "sight" regarding personal obstacles as our blind friends at the Lion's Club were forced to do on their horseback adventure. Trust is extremely difficult, and so another extremely important factor to consider in doing so is in whose criticisms to trust and whose to disregard.

When I first became a mother I would listen to the opinions of every mother that had ever gone before me. I was not arrogant and knew I did not have all the answers so my problem was the opposite. I would listen to *too many* outside opinions regarding my parenting to the detriment of trusting myself. I did this until I realized that for every opinion I received that told me to use cloth diapers I'd get another that told me to use disposable. For every opinion that said a child should be on a strict schedule I heard another that valued letting children's bodies dictate their schedules. I heard disparate opinions on everything from formula to fashion. Eventually, it became painfully obvious I was the one who needed to raise my child and I would be the one to make the decisions about her care. Now this might be a relatively easy thing to do when talking about superficial subjects like clothing or diapers but when it came to discipline it was anything but superficial. As my children grew I recognized I really valued my mother's opinions regarding childrearing. After all, she'd done an excellent job raising me. Didn't she? My mother would most often compliment me on how I was raising my daughters. However, when I was a young mother of about twenty-five, I remember a time when my mother came to visit. I now had a six and a three-year-old daughter. Like many parents, I had somehow become stricter on my firstborn and more lenient on my "baby." This baby girl one day threw a tantrum and my response was extremely lenient. My mother stopped me and said, "Do you realize that had your six-year-old done the same thing that you would have given her much stricter consequences? You would *not* have tolerated her behavior." My mother's words stopped me in my tracks at that moment as I realized she was absolutely right.

What my mother pointed out was, prior to that moment, a blind spot for me. Afterwards, I had a decision to make: do I disagree and disregard her opinion because I didn't like what I was hearing or do I receive the information and make a change? My mother had always given me sound advice. I had learned long ago to trust her opinions for most areas of my life—especially child-rearing. I had learned that my mother's insights could be trusted. I also realized that if I was going to trust her opinions when she agreed with me that I must also trust her opinions when she *disagreed* with me.

When attempting to shrink the *Blind* quadrant we are to look to those persons whose opinions we trust in a particular area (you trust me as a marriage expert) and we should trust that person when they give an opinion we like hearing as well as those we do not like hearing. Not trusting my mother with child-rearing would be in essence an act of arrogance that says "I have no faults." In short, to shrink one's *Blind* quadrant we must respect the opinions of those we trust for truth spoken in love even if what they are revealing is difficult to hear.

Melanie respected my opinion in every other part of her life and even in her marriage when my opinions matched hers. However, she struggled to trust my insights that she had a much larger contribution to the failure of her marriage than she wanted to admit. Melanie needed to trust others enough in order to see herself a bit more clearly. To shrink the *Blind* quadrant we must trust those who love us and care about us.

We cannot trust everyone just as I could not trust the opinions of everyone who tried to tell me how to mother because, as I alluded to in my section above on our *Blind* quadrant, though others may see a part of us that we do not see so, too, do we see a portion of ourselves that they do not. Our job is to find a balance between my perception and theirs.

Consider my earlier example of the friends who called me out on a personal trait that I was, at that time, unaware of. Because I am a deeply self-critical person who is constantly seeking to become a better version of myself, I very quickly and humbly took their perceptions to heart. While there was definitely some truth in *some* of their perceptions (areas I immediately began to improve), I also realized that there were also areas in which their perceptions were largely inaccurate. Our friends and families will not always be one hundred percent correct in their perceptions of us just as my friends were not—because they are imperfect too. They were only partially correct. But *their* knowledge of me had to be balanced with *my* knowledge of me in order to create the most accurate picture possible. While it is arrogant to think everyone else is erroneous, it is also dangerous to *overvalue* others' perceptions to the degree that you lose yourself trying to please them.

Trust is always going to be an issue that we will have to contend with in our intimate relationships. People will entrust different pieces of information with different people and to different degrees depending on the situation. Many couples have eventually shared some of their *Hidden* quadrant with me which then, of course, would cause this information to shift into the *Open* quadrant. "I've had an affair." "I'm addicted to porn." "I'm fearful my spouse will stop loving me because I'm fat." "I've hidden thousands of dollars of credit card debt and am terrified my spouse will find out." Though trust, at its core, is extremely risky, its payoff is of inestimable value in our marriages because trust is essential to build a rich and Super marriage with our spouse. Thus, this research has made one thing blatantly clear: at the very heart of all Super relationships is a deep and spiritual intimacy that gets to the core of the beings involved and ties closely together two once separate persons into one.

Intimacy, the inward, secret, or innermost, is the ultimate product of Superness as it represents a nakedness of one's most private places and speaks of the closeness of knowing another inside and out. Like physical intimacy where another enters our innermost physical places, emotional intimacy allows another to enter our innermost thoughts and feelings and presents a deep personal gift of the self. The richness and ultimate goal of a marriage is to be as intimate as possible "to know me inside and out." The gift is in presenting both the good and flawed parts of the self—the true self—to another to treasure.

Thus, we learn the power of perception in the striving for Super marriages. Super Couples are not Super because they see only the good in their mate but rather because they see all parts of their mate yet choose to *pay focused attention* to those parts that will draw them closer. And when there is a weakness, Super Couples choose to perceive it as a fixable quality or situation rather than perceiving their spouse negatively.

What parts of your spouse do you pay attention to? Do you focus on their strengths or their weaknesses? Do you perceive them as valuable, gifted and talented? Consider your responses and remember that this is the one whom you once saw so wholly good that you vowed to spend the rest of your life with her/him. If you no longer see things the same remember that more likely than not, they haven't changed. Your perspective has. Be Super. Change it back. You'll not regret it.

SC PRINCIPLE #3: COMMUNICATION

We spent considerable time in part two discussing communication, as Super Couples are well aware of its contribution to extremely happy marriages. But before moving on, there is one more part of communication that I'd like to address: emotional intelligence.

Long after I'd finished interviewing and began writing about the Super Couple formula I still felt there was something I was seeing that I was unable to yet articulate. I saw the selflessness, attentiveness, deliberateness in their love, and yet I thought *there's still something different about these Super Husbands that I can't put my finger on.* Unlike the other parts of the Super Couple formula, this one pertained solely to the Husbands. One day it occurred to me that I was witnessing the influence of emotional intelligence on their communication and it immediately made sense.

Everyone has heard of IQ, which measures academic intelligence. It's a set number that increases until approximately age seventeen and then remains relatively stable throughout one's life. According to experts, IQ is only responsible for up to twenty-five percent of success in one's professional and personal life (Kanigan, 2012). However, in the last half century a test has been developed to measure emotional intelligence too. According to Daniel Goleman, EQi is defined as "the capacity for recognizing our own feelings and those of others, for motivating ourselves, and for managing emotions well in ourselves and in our relationships" (1998). Since communication is the process through which we express our thoughts, ideas, and feelings it becomes easy to see why emotional intelligence and communication are so intricately intertwined.

While there is no statistical difference between men and women's *overall* EQ scores, there are particular areas of EQ where women statistically score higher than men—empathy and interpersonal—and it is in these areas that I began to notice the anomaly. According to one group of researchers, "women are more capable of decoding nonverbal emotional information, have greater emotional understanding, are more sensitive to the emotions of others, and are more expressive and show greater interpersonal competencies" (Fernandez-Berrocal et al., 2012, pg 85). But after numerous interviews I noticed a trend among the Super Husbands not apparent in the average male: Super Husbands exhibited a higher than average capacity for empathy and interpersonal relationship.

Empathic people are those who are able to recognize, understand, and appreciate how other people feel. Empathy involves being able to articulate your understanding of another's perspective. Similarly, interpersonal relationship refers to the skill of developing and maintaining mutually satisfying relationships that are characterized by trust and compassion. In most marriages, women are the relationship experts. Based on brain differences already discussed it is easy to understand why, and the Super Wives in this study were no different. Each still exhibited a solid capacity for emotional processing. However, so did their husbands. Each Super Husband seemed to have a keener ability to recognize, understand, and appreciate how their wives were feeling than the average husband, and it was this ability that further allowed for the development of their mutually satisfying relationships.

One particular husband's response illuminated his exceptional capacity for emotional awareness. When asked if he believed others could learn to be super couples Larry asked "*How do you learn maturity and how do you learn feelings because a lot of it is feelings. People without feelings hurt everybody they know. So if you don't have any feelings or empathy for somebody you're going to hurt them. How do you learn that? Can you learn to control your feelings? I think I can. I think I do but I don't know if other people can learn to do it."*

When asked about a time in their marriage they might not have checked the "extremely happy" box Brooke pointed to two situations in their marriage where she would have checked "very unhappy." She acknowledged it was her insecurities about certain situations living abroad. Chuck then responded, *"I don't think it ever got quite that bad for me. I mean I knew it was tense and I knew she was feeling scared but I don't think I even went into unhappy. I always felt like we had a base."* In his statement Chuck quickly recognized and articulated his wife's feelings and then acted on them and calmed her fears.

In responding to Lisa's frustrated moods and not letting it alter his, Jack responded *"I just don't react that way, I love her very much. I try to look at it from her perspective. I try to put myself in her shoes and see. I guess I tend to be more empathetic about that and I don't necessarily take it personally when people yell at me. I try to see why they feel that way...I always try to put myself in the other person's shoes. I don't get upset that much."*

Emotionally aware statements such as these were expressed in one way or another by every super husband, which illuminated their capacity for emotional expression and connection with their wives. I am certain many are now thinking, "Great, my spouse is emotionally unintelligent so there is no chance of us ever becoming a super couple." This includes the emotionally intelligent husband whose wife is the less emotionally intelligent spouse. But do not fret for EQ, unlike IQ, is not stable. Emotional intelligence generally increases with age as it develops over a lifetime of lessons learned and experiences lived. Emotional intelligence *can be* learned! One must simply desire to grow and remain open to self-improvement and change. Just reading this book and actively trying to learn from it can enhance one's relationship and EQ.

One need not be an academic to learn to be more aware of his wife's feelings. The first step in growing emotionally is recognizing this difference in skill sets. The second step is willfully seeking to improve in this area and the third step is to humbly receive the influence of your spouse—listening to, caring about and acting on her feelings. It's not as difficult as one may believe if taken seriously the first three aspects of the super couple formula: put your spouse's emotional needs before your own, be attentive to those needs, and communicate with your spouse about those needs by listening and trusting enough to express your own emotions as well.

There are numerous purveyors of the EQi assessment and if you are interested in personal growth in this area, classes and instructors on emotional intelligence abound. The bottom line is this: to be super in your love for your spouse you must first begin to understand better his/her thoughts and feelings. You must communicate better and more frequently. If you actively seek to do this your spouse will reciprocally grow for you in respect.

SC PRINCIPLE #4: RESPECT

Enough could never be said about the value of and need for respect in our society and culture today. Where it exists, cultures thrive. Where it is absent cultures crumble. Without respect marriages, too, will crumble and dissolve. And they are. We have already delineated many of the problems caused by the absence of respect from our relationships as super couples have universally affirmed that to experience a deeply happy marriage we must choose to respect and esteem our spouses at the highest levels. To reiterate, respecting does not mean agreement but rather is an affirmation of one's worth. As such, respect is such an essential part of the super couple formula that without it not only is happiness not possible but paradoxically contempt fills its void.

Your spouse is an imperfect, broken and flawed individual— but of inestimable worth—like you. If you truly want a super marriage you must choose to esteem your spouse regardless of his/her flaws and failings. Do you not desire to receive the same? Respect is not an option to attain a super marriage. It is a choice you will not regret.

SC PRINCIPLE #5: ENCOURAGEMENT

The power of encouragement is severely underappreciated in society today, especially in our marriages. The untapped power of encouragement greatly deserves our attention as these super couples were epic in their encouragement of one another.

Encouragement was for me an unexpected part of the Super Couple formula. It was not listed as a "main ingredient" in Super Couple marriages when asked. This is not because it is *not* an ingredient but because it was so much a part of their daily lives that to Super Couples it was as automatic as breathing. Listen to these statements from Chuck and Brooke who never mentioned encouragement as a main ingredient:

Brooke: *"I honestly feel like we're better together so why would I screw that up? And why would I ever discount it? I heard this statement, "Stay in awe of your marriage," and I think that it's really true."*

Chuck: *"Even with this Master's Degree thing, I'm so amazed with all of the work that she's doing. She's amazing and it's really cool to take a step back."*

These statements are dripping with encouragement and praise for one another. It's communicated indirectly but ever so powerfully. As with Chuck and Brooke, it soon became obvious that these couples were giving and receiving something I did not see in un-super marriages. As it became apparent I began to question other couples about encouragement in their marriages and they expressed that their spouses were unquestionably their greatest encouragers. But my outsider's perspective allowed a clearer insight to its workings than seen from the inside.

When I first began interviewing I expected to find Super Couples were all optimists. But, as I explained earlier, I found that what I was seeing was not the differences between pessimism and optimism but the differences between encouragement and discouragement. Several super spouses claimed to lean toward pessimism in their general attitudes toward the world and yet, when it came to their marriages those same pessimists were very encouraging of their spouses as well as their dreams, suggestions, possibilities, etc.

We are all capable of moving mountains. We are not fooling ourselves. We really can. Consider ordinary individuals who, in a split second, did extraordinary things like lift a car off of a crushed person because their adrenaline kicked in with no time to rationalize *not accomplishing* such a feat. While we are all capable of moving mountains, lifting cars, or other extraordinary feats, it is easier to believe those capabilities of others than of ourselves. That's where our spouse comes in. Encouragement is one of our spouse's greatest responsibilities: he reminds me I can conquer the world and I remind him of the same. Like accountability partners.

I have this friend. Her name is Crystal. Crystal and I are both women entrepreneurs who left full-time employment to strike out on our own. Every Friday we meet to discuss our successes and focus on next week's goals. While we also talk about unmet goals, etc., our primary focus is on our great and small successes and the opportunities to follow up on during the next week. Our conversations maintain a tone of encouragement because we know intuitively we are each our own greatest discouragers. Why? Because we've already discussed how we are all well aware of our weaknesses and flaws. I don't need *you* to focus on them too. Your greatest gift to me is to make me believe those things about myself that I do not yet believe I am capable of. During these meetings we discuss reasons for unmet goals and then help each other reprioritize next week's goals. I need her encouragement because with every failure or missed opportunity Crystal stops me from beating myself up (though she also prevents too many excuses). That is, she speaks the truth in love.

In the professional sense, Crystal and I fulfill the same roles for each other that spouses should within a marriage. In my experience teaching numerous classes in the professional world (conflict, stress, anger management, leadership and marriage), I have seen how many people believe that to be honest when expressing a criticism means that they must be "tough" without kindness or temperance. And they often sound overly critical. *"What the hell did you think you are doing sliding into work late every freakin' day? I won't put up with crap like that from you or from anyone else in my workplace! Get your act together or you won't have a job to come to next time!"* Being honest and fair are not exclusive from being encouraging. How people criticize can sound hurtful and discouraging, as above, or helpful and encouraging—even when disciplinary action is required. One man who attended a military leadership course I taught once said he had an exceptional boss who would "criticize" in such a manner he would leave feeling encouraged and not even realize he had been reprimanded until after he'd left the meeting. *"Hmm...did I just get chewed out?"* He said the way his boss constructively criticized made him want to work harder for his boss and be a better man. Now *that's* the kind of criticism we should all deliver and receive! There is an art to encouragement and this boss had mastered it.

In the example above, this great boss may have said something like "Look Fred, we need to talk. I've been pretty disappointed with your tardiness at work these days. As you know I have high standards for myself and I hold those same standards for my employees and lately you have not been meeting those standards. I hired you because I believe in you and know you are capable of delivering so much more than you currently are—like that time you found that error in the Metcalf file that ended up saving us $78,000. Though I am going to have to take disciplinary action I do not want you to become discouraged. Let's just consider this a temporary setback. What we're going to do to improve your performance up to your potential is..." Likely, when the employee leaves this office, though he was disciplined, he will leave with a sense of having been encouraged and not discouraged.

In the depths of my soul I have *no problem whatsoever* believing Crystal will one day achieve the high goals she's set for herself and her career. Why couldn't she be a television personality traveling the nation doing food and wine pairings? She is excellent at what she does. When we first began meeting— though she didn't directly express doubts about her vision—they were communicated indirectly. Likely my responses to her ideas were part of what helped propel her forward as she's done for me. My support reminded her I didn't think she was crazy for going after such a "lofty" goal but rather it communicated "I believe in you! If anyone can do this *you* can!" And I meant it. It was genuine confidence.

As a matter of fact I could have never *dreamed* of becoming a public speaker without the encouragement of a friend who believed in me long before I ever believed in myself. Erin met me during a physics class we took while stationed overseas. After getting to know me she asked if I'd develop and deliver a home and car buying seminar for her clients transitioning back into the civilian world. I was terrified as I didn't even have a Bachelor's degree and some of those I'd be speaking to were officers. At first I wavered *"What would I tell them? I've never spoken in public before."* But Erin would not hear of it. She loved my enthusiastic personality and, coupled with my experience "knew" I had what it would take. She believed in me and didn't let me resist. She never let me flounder either. She guided me along the way leading up to the first seminar. She encouraged me at every opportunity. I eventually delivered the seminars and became a regular presenter. From there Erin encouraged me to do Team-Building and Motivational seminars because I was "outstanding" she said. While I thought she was exaggerating to boost my confidence it worked. My confidence in myself grew because someone else first believed in me. I needed Erin's encouragement to even consider standing in front of my first audience let alone one day have a career as a speaker. *"Seriously? Me? I'd rather puke than to speak in front of an audience of ten people!"* Decades later, give me an audience of 20,000 and I thrive. All because someone else first encouraged me.

Our spouses are our lifelong accountability partners. Though they must help us see our blind spots, our spouses are to help us become better versions of ourselves through honest, yet encouraging, feedback. *"Honey you know I want you to have that log cabin in Topeka. I support your dreams because you deserve to be happy and I want your happiness. However, we will never get there if we can't control our spending today. It frustrates me to see the potential for that dream dwindling each time a purchase is made that forces us to dip into our savings."* Super couples go above and beyond that though, as in our next example, by taking what could be perceived as a negative attribute and rephrasing it positively.

In my interview with Chuck and Brooke, we were discussing pessimism and optimism. Since pessimism was perceived less than positively, each somewhat pessimistic spouse would state something to the effect of "Well, I'm really more of a realist." At one point I asked "What would you have called Brooke when you married her? A pessimist or an optimist?"

Chuck: *Working towards optimist. She had her realist moments.*

Brooke: *I was a worrier.*

Chuck: *She was just cautious.*

Even during a moment of potential criticism Chuck took the opportunity to take what Brooke saw as unflattering and put a positive swing on it—not because he was fake or had any ulterior motives—but because he truly believed what he was saying about Brooke. He could have agreed with her "Yeah, she's a pessimist" and likely Brooke would have accepted it. But Super Couples do not do that. They avoid any words that could be perceived as uncomplimentary and turn the criticism into a compliment.

In my interview with Larry and Paula the topic of insecurities came up. Admitting Paula was the only one who initially had any marital insecurities Larry said, "*I think Paula thought I wasn't here for the long run*" to which Paula responded "*Well yeah but also I thought I wasn't good enough. I have an issue that I don't think I'm good enough for certain people. Like I said to Larry, "Anybody can do my job." and he said, "No they can't."* Early on Larry was already encouraging Paula by countering her negative opinions of herself with positive ones. "*One of the biggest things I do,*" continued Larry, "*is I think Paula can do anything that she wants to and I think she's a lot smarter and a lot more talented than she gives herself credit for and she'll start all this kind of self-deprecating stuff and I'll say, "Don't even go there. Your eyes aren't open wide enough to see all the good things about you that I can see and I wish you could. And maybe it's not meant to be but I know it and so maybe you don't even need to know it. You should take my word for it."* Larry and Paula were a beautiful testament to the power of encouragement in fostering extreme marital happiness.

Tricia and Jim were no different. In the following excerpt, Jim details how encouragement manifests in their marriage when he says:

When I was at UVS there was one time where I wanted

to do the best I could. I wanted to be the shooting star of the office. She was like, "Well, you can! You're gonna do this and you're gonna work hard" and all that stuff. As I was working, I found out I was going to be promoted to vice-president and I was going to be the youngest one in Virginia Beach. So, I remember telling her that and she was like, "I knew you could!" It was just huge. It was so cool. There's a certain amount more business I had to do before I knew I could make it, and I did. But she was always like, "You can do it! You can do it! Just keep working." I'm a very self-motivated person anyway. The nice thing is, when I get focused on something, it's not necessarily that she's encouraging; it's that she's not discouraging. So, if I see a goal, and it's important to me, she will encourage me no matter what and not discourage me. She's phenomenal, and I don't know if I'm good about that or not but I think I'm okay. Sometimes I wonder if my language comes across as not encouraging. I think that I am not as good as an encourager as she is. Sometimes I think of myself as a realist I guess instead of just an optimist.

Tricia responded: *I don't think he has ever discouraged me from anything, he only encourages me. Not only in my job, my family that I grew up in, and in my friends. I don't think there has ever been a time where he has discouraged me from something.*

Rob is an Ironman Triathlete who runs races quite regularly. And while she is not overly competitive, Maggie is always there to cheer him on. But while Rob greatly appreciates Maggie's support and encouragement on race day he reciprocates his as well. When Maggie enters the occasional race, Rob will not run it too. He said, *"Like with my races...she'll go to every one. And I'll go out there if she wants to race. I won't run the race so that I'm not competing against her. You know what I mean? I mean I'd do the same race but then it's not her race. You know, so it's her. That's her day to do whatever she wants."*

"You mean you don't run with her so you can support her and not compete against her?"

"Well I wouldn't be competing against her but I wouldn't be focused on her achievement for that day."

And for Rob taking any of the focus from Maggie's accomplishments was unacceptable when he could be there to encourage her instead.

As with every Super Couple, Maggie and Rob, like Tricia and Jim or Larry and Paula, are each other's biggest cheerleaders. While this, like the other parts of the formula, may seem absolutely obvious, encouragement is not usually found in troubled marriages as it is usually replaced with discouragement that tears the other down instead. While it might seem intentional or mean to discourage one's spouse, it is not always blatant or recognizable. This was true of my own marriage decades ago. Before I realized what an amazing handyman my young husband was I recall him asking whether he should do a particular home repair himself or hire a handyman. It was a relatively large and expensive task and I remember saying we should probably hire someone to ensure it was done right. Looking back I now recognize that my husband was seeking my encouragement to give him the added confidence he needed to undertake the task. While there was no intent to hurt or deflate my husband, my discouraging response conveyed that I didn't fully believe in his abilities. In that response I failed.

Encouragement and discouragement are very powerful forces. While the former helps to propel us forward; the latter holds us back and hinders our success by discouraging even the smallest attempt. Consider the current but faulty notion of the divorce rate being at or near fifty percent. If you are a young couple considering marriage would *you* be encouraged by this statistic to do so? Likely not. So many are discouraged that fewer opt to marry than in past decades. But what if you heard the truth that actually less than four of ten couples divorce—that most marriages succeed? Would you be more encouraged that your own marriage would succeed? Of course you would. It is human nature to look to those who have gone before us to show us a particular endeavor is possible.

It used to be said that a four-minute mile was impossible for the human body to run—that it was physiologically incapable of doing so. On May 6, 1954, Roger Bannister became the first man to do so. Soon thereafter, twenty-four others did the same. Why? Because Bannister's success encouraged others to believe they too could accomplish the same feat. Knowing more couples succeed at marriage than fail likewise encourages others to push forward rather than give up when times get tough. Further, the whole purpose of this book—proving that an extremely happy marriage is possible for all who endeavor to attain one—was to encourage any who read it that they, too, can become a Super Couple. I have been told numerous times that the fact my marriage survived was encouraging to couples who had lost hope for their own marital success. More than once I've had a couple say to me "Because your marriage survived I *know* mine can too!" Nothing blesses me more than to hear that. Encouragement is reciprocal. Like with the four minute mile, the numerous examples of those whose marriages have attained extreme happiness are encouraging to those of us who now have hope of the same. So be encouraged! Super is well within your grasp!

Now that we know a super marriage is attainable for anyone who understands and implements the formula, there remains one last important component that ties it all together.

SC PRINCIPLE #6: DELIBERATENESS

At the end of my interview with Chuck and Brooke I asked why it seemed so easy for them to each put their spouse before themselves. Brooke responded, "*Christine, we are human. We are just as selfish as anybody else. It's just that each morning we have to make a conscious choice to be selfless to one another.*" Her husband concurred, "*I think when you first get married it's a whole new world. You control your thoughts and your thinking and I think just learning to put the other person before yourself. It takes a while.*"

So selflessness is deliberate?

Tricia and Jim—known to friends as "Team Sexy"—were asked about the work involved in pleasing one's spouse on a daily basis. Tricia corrected by interjecting, "*Christine, I really don't like to use the word work, but rather effort. Work implies pain and I don't find it painful at all to try to please Jim and meet his needs.*" Tricia wasn't alone. This sentiment was expressed by every couple in some way.

Before I began this research I truly believed Super Couples were super by luck. They married the "right person" and from then on their love was effortless. Knowing now how wrong I was has made writing this book a joy. Knowing the true reason for these super marriages was not because these couples "had" something special but because they "did" something special was the ultimate proof super was not reserved for the fortunate few. Superness is possible for every married couple that deliberately sets out to attain it. Super Couples choose to be selfless each and every day. They pay attention to their spouses' strengths rather than focusing on their flaws. *"My spouse is not a bad person. He/she is just having a bad day."* Super Couples communicate frequently and lovingly with one another in ways that are patient, kind, and not rude. They communicate in ways that show their respect, esteem and adoration. They encourage one another— and they do all this deliberately. With Super Couples, as with all of us, love is a choice.

Brooke said we should be mindful of one another which she certainly is. This means we cannot nonchalantly act on emotion as we effortlessly did in the first months of our relationships. Mindfulness means just that—engaging our minds to consider our thoughts, words and actions toward our spouses. Mindfulness means deliberately thinking through our options when we interact with loved ones. Chuck thought it through and said *"Brooke is the most amazing woman I ever dated and then I married her. I'm not messing this up."*

Super does not come naturally—it is actively sought.

Mindfulness takes effort. Though initially it seemed daily mindfulness would be exhausting, Super Couples have assured us it is not. Like any other habit one sets out to acquire, over time loving deliberately becomes easier, more natural and less effortful. Actively loving becomes pleasurable to the lover— habitual. *"Do you have to work to stay happily married?* I asked. *"I think we individually work hard"* Lisa said. *"But for other people they have to work hard for their marriage to work. It's not like that for us, it's very natural. I just want to make him happy and that's not work."*

Thank you Lisa. That's exactly what we were hoping to hear.

Some Final Truths

UNCONDITIONAL LOVE

Is it possible to love unceasingly? What about loving without conditions?

When I teach pre-marital classes I query my students about many aspects of their future marriages. I do so to open their minds to areas of marriage they likely never considered. Though preparing for marriage, few expect to hear instruction focused on divorce yet I'd be doing a disservice if I did not get them thinking about it. After all, avoiding divorce and sustaining a thriving marriage are the same feat. I begin by asking if they love their fiancé. Of course they look at me as if I have two heads as if to say "Well, of course. Duh. Isn't that a no-brainer? But where are you going with this?" Then, when asked "How do you know?" they say "because he/she tells me so" to which I respond "Well I love you. Do you believe me?" Of course none of them does. Point made. Anyone can *say* they love you. Not everyone can show it. So then I ask, "How now do you *know* your fiancé' loves you? And why do you love them? And they begin to list all the reasons they love their mate. "He holds the door for me." "She's there for me when I need her." "He listens when I talk." And so on. Then I ask *"Is there anything your fiancé could ever do to make you stop loving him/her?"* Most say no until one brave soul pipes up and says *"Only if he/she has an affair"* to which I respond *"Then you're not ready for marriage."* That silences a room in a millisecond.

An affair. Now there's a condition. Painful, yes. Devastating, absolutely. But a condition nonetheless. *You've crossed a line there buddy and I'm done. I rescind my love right here and now!*

So what are the conditions of *your* love? Are there conditions? Or are you willing to say "I will never, ever divorce my spouse"? In this new millennium of no-fault divorces there are very few who actually believe in unconditional love, at least for our spouses. Most claim unconditional love for our children. And for the most part, loving our children is about as close as we can naturally come to "unconditional" love. Many a parent has spent hours in the prison visiting room to "love" a child that erred terribly in the eyes of the law. Why is that parent still at the side of the child?

Love.

Husbands and wives will endure tough seasons where one or both stop "loving" the other: a particular day or during a fight. When you make a sarcastic or rude remark to your spouse you have stopped loving. When you impatiently wait for her to join you in the car for an event you'll be late to and then lay on the horn loudly in disgust you have stopped loving her. When you speak unkindly you have stopped loving. In those few short seconds where you thought to yourself "I hate him!" you had, in fact, stopped loving. Love is an action. Saying "I hate you" is unloving. Loving without ceasing is just not possible for humans. Humans don't like to be hurt. And hurting is often a side-effect of love. Hurt me and I'll hurt you back.

So can we love unconditionally?

Though we say at the altar "until death do us part, in good times and bad," few really mean that anymore. When the bad times come we're outta there. The bad times suck. Sometimes they *really* suck. We all want to impose conditions on how, when and why we will love another and most of those conditions have to do with *me* and *my* happiness. Once I stop being happy I stop loving unconditionally. Ironically, though we find it difficult to love another unconditionally, we still desire *to be loved* as such. *"I'm only human after all. I'm not perfect. Geez, what does he expect?!"* So of course it was a matter of great curiosity to find out what super couples felt about unconditional love.

Jack: *That's the love I feel for her and I think that's the love we have from God. I think the blessing is that when you accept that unconditional love from God and you feel secure in it, then you can give that unconditional love to others. That's how I feel about Lisa and our children. So no matter what they do and no matter how horrible my kids behave, I always love them unconditionally. If I don't like their actions, I still love them unconditionally.*

About an hour ago I was on the phone with another client struggling in his marriage. He desperately wants to save his marriage of three years and yet recently his wife said she no longer loved him and wants them to just be friends. He is at his wits end trying to win her heart back. He is soul searching to try to become a better version of himself than he was before. He is treating her with a renewed affection and attention to her needs and is even in the middle of *The Love Dare*—a challenge to selflessly put his wife's needs before his own. In his mind he is doing everything he can and nothing is working, which is why he contacted me. After listening to his story it became apparent his wife is exhibiting the signs of one in the midst of an affair. So when I asked, "Do you think she's having an affair?" he answered "Well, I asked her and she said no. I don't think she is." I then posed this question "What if she admitted she were? What would you do?" He pondered his response and then said, "Well, I guess I'd divorce her."

One minute earlier this man was willing to do "anything" to win his wife back but in fact he was untruthful. His love had conditions. "I'll love you only unless…"

Why is it so difficult to stand for our marriages? Why is our first inclination to run once we are hurt by those we love? Why do so many choose "flight" over "fight"? Why is forgiveness so hard?

STANDING FOR MARRIAGE

In August of this year my husband and I celebrated our thirty-second wedding anniversary and I must say I am extremely happy to report that because less than a decade ago I wanted nothing more than a second chance to "do it right" with the next guy—whoever that might be. Twenty-eight years ago *I* was the one who left him for another man in pursuit of finding "true love." I did not. Well, at least not with the other man. But I did, in fact, find true love: with the man who'd refused to give up on this prodigal and stood by his commitment to love me until death departed us. My husband was a Stander and for that I praise God daily.

Was my husband a better person than other victims of infidelity or marital trauma? Maybe. But maybe not. Why did our marriage survive while so many others fail? My answer to all is the same: only by the grace of God did our marriage survive—the same grace that will carry your marriage through the bad times to the good as well.

Although we had no idea when we first married, (we barely knew each other after only two and a half months together), my husband and I are both people of deep faith. And although we also weren't going to church or practicing our faith when we married, we both loved the Lord. We just weren't really paying any attention to Him at that point. We were both pursuing our own selfish endeavors and putting little thought into actually "doing" anything to stay happily married. We didn't know we had to. And for that I am deeply regretful. I wish desperately someone had taken the time to teach us how to be married, show us the formula, mentor us, chastise us (when necessary), and hold us to our vows. Few, it seems, are willing to do that anymore for fear of getting into someone else's private "business." "*I saw Sally totally embarrass her husband today. It was so disrespectful. Oh well, it's not my business. I don't want to be considered a know-it-all so I'm not saying a word.*"

Why not? Since when are we as a community okay with sitting back, watching another get hurt and looking the other way? Had we witnessed a purse being stolen would we have not intervened? Of course we would have! The difference is that everyone accepts purse snatching as a bad thing and feels it socially acceptable to defend the victim from being wronged. When it comes to relationships few speak up because we don't all agree on what right and wrong are (out loud, that is). But what about the disrespectful wife in our example? Was it not also our business to pull Sally privately aside and "speak the truth in love" to her? To guide her? To teach her? When I selfishly left my husband so many years ago no one "called me out" on my awful choice, but I wish they had. Their silence conveyed acceptance and made it easier for me to blame only Dan and not myself.

And I nearly devastated the lives of two innocent daughters. Our choices are much bigger than ourselves and no matter what others tell us, our choices affect entire communities.

My focus, however, is not on what contributes to marital failures but rather marital successes. Like my husband so many years ago, our job as spouses is to work through trials with as much unconditional love as possible. We must surrender our pride, our egos, our embarrassment and do that which we vowed to do when we stood at the altar. You're likely thinking it's easy for me to say as I wasn't the one "left" but was, rather, the leaver. But alas, it is not easy to say because even the leaver has to deal with a lot of pain and emotion as well: embarrassment, pride, hurt, guilt, shame, remorse—and all the consequences that come with that poor choice. Ultimately, Dan and I were both Standers, we just never realized it...until now.

I praise God because during our four-year separation Dan returned to the Lord and church, and made the decision to pursue me again—the one who'd humiliated him—because before God and man he'd vowed to do so. Dan squelched his ego and his pride and set out "to love" me again. And it was very attractive. While I seek in no way to blame my actions on my husband for I alone take responsibility for my choices, Dan realized that he, too, was responsible for some poor choices of his own prior to my leaving him and for those he, too, was sorry. He began to call more often, to speak kindly again, to pursue me again. During that same season I, too, had returned to church, deepened my prayer life, began attending mass again and, most of all, repented. Eventually I submitted to Dan's loving actions and made the decision to recommit my love to my husband. As I stood in my living room in 1990 I remember thinking to myself *"Okay Christine, the first time you got married you were 18, pregnant and stupid. Everyone would have understood had you divorced. But this time you are 26, know what you're getting into, and willingly entering this decision to remain married. This time you have no excuse. This time it's for life."*

I'll never forget that day because I have come to realize through these Super Couples that that simple recommitment to love my husband until the day one of us leaves this earth was, coupled with our attempts to love, what allowed this marriage to survive and thrive. I cannot stress enough that if you are reading this book that your marriage, too, can thrive if you refuse to give up! Please, DO NOT give up on your marriage! Do not give up on your children's marriage! Do not give up on your neighbor's marriage! FIGHT for it! Fight for your marriage and fight for theirs! Fight for your children's and your grandchildren's security! They're crying out to us to please show them how to deal with conflict! *"Mom and Dad, show us that we're worth fighting for!"*

Divorce is ever so tempting when we are hurting. Do not succumb to the temptation if you have not exhausted every other avenue for marital reparation: retreats, counseling, mentoring, prayer, and, most importantly, God.

I love reporting that fifty percent of couples that survive infidelity go on to have thriving marriages. Why? Because they realize what they almost lost. Prodigal spouses very often learn from their mistakes yet don't get to reap the rewards of those lessons because the offended spouse quits and moves on because they were unwilling to forgive or afraid of being hurt again. Standers learn lessons too. Had they worked through the affairs and the troubles, their new and improved marriage to their original spouse is nearly always better than they could have imagined before the affair or traumatic event. Marriages only fail when *both* spouses quit. When one spouse lovingly "fights" for the other it can't help but be attractive because love is always attractive.

So that's my love story. No, we weren't a perfect couple. We never will be. None of these couples is. But I can tell you right now that we, too, will one day be a Super Couple. How do I know that? Because love is an action and we are committed to *doing* all the loving things we possibly can for each other. We are committed to doing our best to be patient, kind, not rude, not jealous, not quick to anger and will no longer keep record of wrongs. We are committed to seeking the interests of the other and surrendering the needs of the self. And we know that this *SACRED* formula is foolproof. So love one another and you too, will live *extremely* happily ever after.

Love is patient, love is kind. It is not jealous, [love] is not pompous, it is not inflated, it is not rude, it does not seek its own interests, it is not quick-tempered, it does not brood over injury, it does not rejoice over wrongdoing but rejoices with the truth. It bears all things, believes all things, hopes all things, endures all things.

Love never fails. 1 Cor. 13: 4-8

REFERENCES

Bentley, P. (2011, March 4). Why an arranged marriage 'is more likely to develop into lasting love'. *Daily mail. com,* Retrieved from http://www.dailymail.co.uk/news/ article-1363176/Why-arranged-marriage-likely-develop-lasting-love.html

Brizendine, L. (2006). *The female brain.* New York: Broadway Books.

Brizendine, L. (2010). *The male brain.* New York: Broadway Books.

Fernandez-Berrocal, P., Cabello, R., Castillo-Gualda, R. & Extremera, N. (2012). Gender differences in emotional intelligence: The mediating effect of age. *Behavioral Psychology,* 20 (1), 77-89.

Goleman, D. (1995). *Emotional intelligence: Why it can matter more than IQ.* New York: Bantam.

Gottman Institute Web site http://www.gottman.com/research/ research-faqs/

Gungor, M. (2011, February 28). *A Tale of Two Brains* [Video file]. Retrieved from https://www.youtube.com/ watch?v=3XjUFYxSxDk.

Happiness. (2015, July 19). Retrieved from http://greatergood. berkeley.edu/topic/happiness/definition

Hastings, J. (1914). Hedonism. In *Encyclopedia of Religion and Ethics.* (Vol. 6, pp. 567-568). New York: Charles Scribner's Sons.

Hedonism. (2015, November 9). *Wikipedia*, s.v. Retrieved from https://en.m.wikipedia.org/wiki/Hedonism.

Kahneman, D, & Deaton, A. (2010). High income improves evaluation of life but not emotional well-being. *Proceedings of the National Academy of Sciences,* 107 (38), 16489-16493.

Kanigan, D. (2012, Mar 9). 25% of job success is predicted by IQ 75% is predicted by your optimism levels. *Live & Learn,* Retrieved from http://davidkanigan. com/2012/03/09/25-of-job-success-is-predicted-by-i-q-75-is-predicted-by-your-optimism-levels/

Kelly, M. (2010). *Rediscover catholicism: A spiritual guide to living with passion and purpose.* (2nd ed.). Boston, MA: Beacon.

Larimore, W. & Larimore, B. (2008). *His brain, her brain: How divinely designed differences can strengthen your marriage.* Grand Rapids: Zondervan.

Love. (1884). In *Webster's condensed dictionary: Etymologies, definitions, pronunciations and spelling with appendix and illustrations.* New York & Chicago: Ivison, Blakeman, Taylor, and Co.

Love. (1920). In *The desk standard dictionary of the English language.* New York & London: Funk and Wagnalls.

Love. (1956). In *Webster's new collegiate dictionary: Based on Webster's new international dictionary.* Springfield, MA: G. & C. Merriam Co.

Love. (1964). In *Webster's new world dictionary of the American language: College edition.* Cleveland & New York: World Publishing Company.

Love. (1982). In *The American heritage dictionary of the English language: New college edition*. Boston: Houghton Mifflin.

Love. (2012, Dec. 6). In *A dictionary of the English language: A digital edition of the 1755 classic by Samuel Johnson. "Page View, Pages 1229-1230."* Retrieved from http:// johnsonsdictionaryonline.com/?page_id=7070&i=1229.

Luft, J. & Ingham, H. (1955). The Johari window, a graphic model of interpersonal awareness. *Proceedings of the western training laboratory in group development*, Los Angeles: University of California, Los Angeles.

Lyubomirsky, S. (2007). *The how of happiness: A scientific approach to getting the life you want*. New York, NY: Penguin Press.

Marsh, J. (2010, July 21). The hows of happiness: Seven research-tested strategies for a happier life. *Greater Good*. Retrieved from http://greatergood.berkeley.edu/ article/item/the_hows_of_happiness

Statistics brain, (2012, December 1). *Arranged marriage statistics*. Retrieved from http://www.statisticbrain. com/arranged-marriage-statistics/

CPSIA information can be obtained
at www.ICGtesting.com
Printed in the USA
BVHW071204251121
622517BV00008B/250

9 781633 932012